PRAISE FOR *WHEN G...*

"Whether you're preaching to a church or ... presence is an intimidating topic. *When God Isn't There will prove useful in* either setting. I've worked with David before, and his talents as a spoken word poet serve him just as well in written form. He wrestles with theological concepts in a down-to-earth way. I believe many will benefit from this very helpful book."

—Kyle Idleman, bestselling author of *Not a Fan*;
teaching pastor, Southeast Christian Church,
Louisville, Kentucky

"I struggle to describe this book, not because it is incoherent (far from it) but because it is so richly diverse. It is saturated with Scripture, personal experience, analogies and metaphors drawn from every sphere of life, outrageously funny stories, illustrations that make complex truths meaningful, and, on top of it all, really good theology. David's book has breathed new life into my favorite biblical text: 'In your presence is fullness of joy; at your right hand are pleasures forevermore' (Ps. 16:11). Trust me, it's a page-turner. And a life changer. Highly recommended!"

—Sam Storms, PhD, lead pastor for Teaching and
Vision, Bridgeway Church, Oklahoma City, Oklahoma

"Nothing debilitates us more than distance from God. *When God Isn't There* weaves poetry and prose into an insightful exploration of God's presence, revealing the enduring comfort we can find when we embrace his full nature. A gifted artist rooted in the truth and beauty of Scripture, David has created a must-read for anyone who's felt far from God."

—Bobby Gruenewald, LifeChurch Innovation Leader
and a founder of YouVersion

"Some people fake the presence of God in their lives because secretly they want to fit in. But when they are alone they wonder, *Where is God*? Why do others seem to feel his presence and I do not? Whether you feel that now or have never felt it, David Bowden explores this important topic with honesty and poetic vision. *When God Isn't There* will comfort you, deepening your understanding of God's presence right now."

—Mark Matlock, WisdomWorks

"David Bowden's *When God Isn't There* is utterly praiseworthy. Every chapter amplifies the truth about the deep ache and joy that marks the life of a Christ follower. Bowden gives us a new language for communicating the tension between God's holy presence and sometimes-painful absence. This book indeed reveals how God is farther than you think and closer than you dare to imagine."

—Tami Heim, president and CEO, Christian
Leadership Alliance

"Wycliffe USA's work of Bible translation often brings us to places around the world where it feels as though God is absent because his Word is not available in the language people know and understand best. *When God Isn't There* is a timely, insightful, and inspiring reminder that God is always present and always at work."

—Bob Creson, president and CEO, Wycliffe Bible
Translators USA

"I've had the privilege of knowing and working with David for several years, and he is an outstanding thinker and communicator. His passion for God's Word, his command of the Scriptures, and his winsome life are assets God has at his disposal as he seeks to advance his kingdom and build Jesus Church here on earth! David's transparency in addressing this age-old question for humanity will help all to better understand that God's seeming absence is actually an invitation to seek him wholeheartedly and that in doing so one will find him."

—J. Todd Peterson, chairman emeritus, Seed
Company; NFL placekicker, 1993–2005

"Natalie, nails, idols, Mouse Trap, Proclaimer Boxes, pursuing the love of your life, Corvettes, goats, erasers, five-dollar bills, temple robbers. Absence, presence, darkness, suffering. Abraham, Moses, Job, Jonah, Jesus, Mother Teresa. In *When God Isn't There*, Bowden weaves together the subjects above to paint a vivid picture of God's seeming absence and real presence in our lives. Reading this little book reminded me that God's presence is about God, not me. It made me contemplate that perhaps there are things in my life that I need to absent myself from to be more present with God. It reminded me that God is everywhere, not just in a church building on Sunday mornings. This book is a great reminder that we are created to glorify God and enjoy him forever."

—Dr. Dudley Chancey, PhD, professor of Youth
Ministry, Oklahoma Christian University

WHEN
GOD
ISN'T
THERE

WHEN

GOD

ISN'T

THERE

WHY GOD IS FARTHER THAN YOU THINK,
BUT CLOSER THAN YOU DARE IMAGINE

DAVID BOWDEN

NELSON
BOOKS

An Imprint of Thomas Nelson

Published in Nashville, Tennessee, by Nelson Books, an imprint of Thomas Nelson. Nelson Books and Thomas Nelson are registered trademarks of HarperCollins Christian Publishing, Inc.

The author is represented by Alive Literary Agency, 7680 Goddard Street, Suite 200, Colorado Springs, Colorado 80920, www.aliveliterary.com.

Thomas Nelson titles may be purchased in bulk for educational, business, fund-raising, or sales promotional use. For information, please e-mail SpecialMarkets@ThomasNelson.com.

Unless otherwise noted, Scripture quotations are taken from The Holy Bible, English Standard Version® (ESV®), copyright © 2001 by Crossway, a publishing ministry of Good News Publishers. Used by permission. All rights reserved.

Scripture quotations marked NIV are from the Holy Bible, New International Version®, NIV®. Copyright © 1973, 1978, 1984, 2011 by Biblica, Inc.® Used by permission of Zondervan. All rights reserved worldwide. www.zondervan.com. The "NIV" and "New International Version" are trademarks registered in the United States Patent and Trademark Office by Biblica, Inc.®

Scripture quotations marked NASB are from New American Standard Bible®. Copyright © 1960, 1962, 1963, 1968, 1971, 1972, 1973, 1975, 1977, 1995 by The Lockman Foundation. Used by permission. (www.Lockman.org)

Scripture quotations marked NLT are from the Holy Bible, New Living Translation. © 1996, 2004, 2007, 2013 by Tyndale House Foundation. Used by permission of Tyndale House Publishers, Inc., Carol Stream, Illinois 60188. All rights reserved.

ISBN 9780718077686 (eBook)

Library of Congress Cataloging-in-Publication Data

Names: Bowden, David, 1987- author.
Title: When God isn't there : why God is farther than you think, but closer than you dare imagine / David Bowden.
Description: Nashville : Thomas Nelson, 2016.
Identifiers: LCCN 2016004441 | ISBN 9780718077631
Subjects: LCSH: Hidden God. | Spirituality--Christianity. | God (Christianity)--Knowableness. | Spiritual life--Christianity.
Classification: LCC BT180.H54 B69 2016 | DDC 231.7--dc23 LC record available at https://lccn.loc.gov/2016004441

Printed in the United States of America
16 17 18 19 20 21 RRD 6 5 4 3 2 1

For Meagan: the one who reminds me, in word, deed, and prayer, that God is never too far.

Now to him who is able to keep you from stumbling and to present you blameless before the presence of his glory with great joy.

—Jude 1:24

CONTENTS

Introduction   xi

SECTION 1: WHY GOD ISN'T THERE   1

   Chapter 1: Hummers and Birthstones   5
     Why does God feel so absent?

   Chapter 2: Trash Bag Covered Walls   11
     Why does God have to be absent?

   Chapter 3: God: Absent and Everywhere   29
     Isn't God always present?

SECTION 2: CHASING OUR ABSENT GOD   41

   Chapter 4: The Moses Principle: More Wants More   45
     Why does God feel farther the closer I get?

   Chapter 5: The Far-Off Promises of an Elusive God   61
     Why must Christians wait?

   Chapter 6: Sick with Love   81
     How do I search for a God who is absent?

CONTENTS

SECTION 3: THE CHURCH AND GOD'S PRESENCE   99

Chapter 7: When God Stops Coming to Church   103
If God left, would you notice?

Chapter 8: Where Two or Three Are Gathered   123
Where is God in worship?

SECTION 4: AFFLICTION, ABANDONMENT, AND ABSENCE   137

Chapter 9: Presence in Suffering   141
Is God present when we suffer?

Chapter 10: That Safe Darkness   161
Where is God in the darkness?

SECTION 5: THE GOSPEL OF NEARNESS   175

Chapter 11: God with Us   179
How should I understand the presence of Jesus?

Chapter 12: Present for Absence   193
How did Jesus defeat absence?

Chapter 13: The Spirit and Absence   211
Is God absent if he lives in me?

Chapter 14: Sooner Than We Deserve, but Not
As Soon As We Desire   231
What will eternal presence and absence be like?

Acknowledgments   247

Notes   249

About the Author   258

INTRODUCTION

*Beloved, we are God's children now, and
what we will be has not yet appeared; but we
know that when he appears we shall be like
him, because we shall see him as he is.*

—1 JOHN 3:2

The presence of God is confusing. I'm sure many of us have asked questions about what God's presence means at one time or another. How can he be everywhere at once but dwell in heaven? If a good God is present in this world, why is there suffering? How can God be present with believers but absent to nonbelievers? If he is supposed to live inside me, why does he often feel far from me? What do we mean when we say God is present? For that matter, what do we mean when we say God is absent? Are we even allowed to ask that question?

The spirituality offered by our world tells us that God is everywhere and that we simply need to have more faith to be able to experience his nearness. But such clichés don't change the fact that our hearts and minds are often filled with turmoil, doubt, and shame because of how absent God can feel to us. Most of the advice and resources we are given when going through a season of God's absence are just reassurances about his presence. These are helpful, good, and well intentioned, but why don't we speak directly to the absence of God? I think it's because talking about an absent God is taboo.

But God's absence is not a taboo subject for the Bible.

Like the vast majority of Christians, I went through a long period of feeling like God was far away from me. I was in college getting my Bible degree, and God's presence seemed thin to me at best and a joke to me at worst. The most insufferable part about this time was that there seemed to be no one to talk to. Either people couldn't relate to what I was going through, or they were going through it so deeply themselves that they were unable to be of any real help.

Every time I prayed, I could have sworn that only the walls were listening. Every time I picked up my Bible, all I saw was ink and paper. Every time I went to church, all I felt was ritual and tradition. Everyone was telling me God was with me, but I had a hard time believing it because I couldn't feel him for myself.

After a long time, the season of absence passed. It didn't happen overnight, but moved slowly, inch by inch, like a sunrise encroaching over the horizon. After college I began to become fascinated all over again with this idea of God's presence and absence, so I set out to study what the Bible had to say about God's absence. What I found was shocking. The Bible is full of God's absence. Even though it is a book about God's presence, there is still ample talk of absence. I immediately realized this must be vastly more important than how little it is talked about.

I began to extend my research of God's presence and absence to sources outside of the Bible and was even more surprised by what

I found there—almost nothing. What I was able to find within theological circles was that this concept is referred to as "Divine Absence," and more non-Christians seem to have written about it as a literary exercise than Christians as a theological necessity.

As I began to dig deeper, I saw the language and reality of Divine Absence everywhere: from Adam to Moses, the Psalms to the Prophets, and even Jesus and his disciples. I found that not only could God be absent but that God was absent many times throughout Scripture. Why was nobody talking about this? Since so many of us often feel far from God, wouldn't understanding what Scripture says about his absence be crucial?

After about four years of studying this material on my own, I was approached about writing a book. The wonderful woman who would become my friend and literary agent asked if I had anything I wanted to write about, and God's absence was burning at the tip of my tongue.

I know what it is like to feel like God has abandoned you. Coming from a broken home, I've felt the sting of absence and the desperation of loss. I know what it's like to almost scream at the walls of your room in prayer, hoping that something will escape them and get to God's ear, even though you're pretty certain he's not listening. I know what it is like to be bombarded with feelings of distance only to be handed fluffy platitudes of nearness.

So if you will allow me to walk you through the journey that I have been on, I will show you what the Bible has to say about God's absence and how these truths actually lead us into a sweeter experience of and a desire for his presence.

I will show you that God feels absent because he is present. We will walk through why God must be absent and why his absence is actually a form of grace. You will see how it is possible for God to be present everywhere yet still be absent all around us. We'll see why the closer we draw to God, the farther he feels. I'll tell you about how God uses absence and presence to orchestrate the events of the world and draw more desire and love out of us.

We will take a look at our churches and worship services and see how we can properly understand God's presence and absence within those settings. You will discover how absence relates to pain and suffering as well as spiritual darkness. Finally, I will demonstrate to you how the gospel simultaneously defeats absence while still increasing our experience of it.

God is absent in the way we most desire but present in the way we most require. This is the mystery we will uncover throughout this book: why God is not here, and why he is never going away. I pray this journey breaks down barriers in your mind and heart and lets you see that God is farther than you think and closer than you dare to imagine.

WHY GOD ISN'T THERE

Always. Usually. Maybe. Never.

God is always absent.
God is usually absent.
God may be absent.
God is never absent.

All four of these statements are true.
All four of these statements are true at the same time.
All four of these statements are true at the same time without
*   any contradiction.*

Always.
Usually.
Maybe.
Never.

And the only way we will ever
Come to terms with this
Idea, which is seemingly inconsistent,

Is if we give up the preconception
That our God is static.

Because sometimes God is present
And sometimes God is absent.
And at all times he is all things
Because God is always dynamic.

He can be nowhere on earth, yet is omnipresent.
He can choose to be transparent to one, but to another be
  resplendent.
He can be itinerant in some respects, and, yet, in others be a
  resident.
He is the transcendent Father who, in his Son, is immensely
  imminent.

God's presence and absence
May seem to be in competition
But that is only because we are viewing them
With the limits of our own cognition.

For

God is not physically here right now—
He is always absent in his actuality.

God is not often seen with human eyes—
He is usually absent in his visibility.

God is not present with the lost as he is with the saved—
He may be absent relationally.

But God is present in his sustaining power—
God is never absent generally.

And what causes this perceived contradiction is, in fact, God's
consistency.
What creates a schism in our minds really comes from God's
uniformity.

It is his uncompromising justice
And his endless, inexhaustible grace
That create this present and this absent state.

For if he stayed
Present in the way
He did in Eden's garden
Then fallen humanity as we know it
Would have long since departed.

So his absence is grace
As is his continuing presence.
For he didn't stay and destroy us
Nor did he abandon us at our sin's first occurrence.

His absence is kindness,
Yet his presence did not retire.

For without the former we would be abolished,
Without the latter we would expire.

He withdrew to preserve us
But stayed near so that his plan might transpire

Because
God is absent in the way we most desire
But present in the way we most require.

So he is always absent but present forever.

Always.
Usually.
Maybe.
Never.

ONE

HUMMERS AND BIRTHSTONES

Why does God feel so absent?

He has planted eternity in the human heart,
but even so, people cannot see the whole scope
of God's work from beginning to end.
—ECCLESIASTES 3:11 (NLT)

I was speaking at a conference in Tennessee where about twenty-two thousand teenagers were gathered to worship God and hear lessons from his Word. If you've ever been to anything like this, you may know how encouraging it is to be completely surrounded by so many like-minded people who are proclaiming the same truths as you. However, you may also know how alone you can feel when everyone around you seems to be fully convinced and content in their praise, while you feel detached and dissatisfied in yours. Such was the case for a seventeen-year-old girl named Natalie who approached me after I spoke.

I had just finished performing a poem on stage and had made my way back to my booth to chat with some of the teens. Without a preamble, handshake, or pleasantry, Natalie came right up to me and asked, "How do you know God is real?" Due to the suddenness and depth of the question, I was a little rattled.

After gaining my composure, I sought to garner a little more insight. "Why do you ask?" I questioned back.

Her response crystallized in my mind a key aspect of God's absence. Eyes replete with both conviction and sorrow, Natalie said, "Everyone is in there singing about how they can see and feel the glory of God. But all I see is a stadium and all I feel is absence." Natalie, in her pain and honesty, boldly articulated the ache many of us hide in our hearts. God feels absent. Sometimes it feels like God isn't there.

Perhaps you are like Natalie in some way. You may not feel like you are connecting with the most high God when you go to church on Sunday. You may hear all the songs and the messages being proclaimed, yet feel like you are missing out on something so obvious. "What's wrong with me?" is more often on your lips than the worship songs.

But what if feeling God's absence could be a faith builder instead of a faith breaker? What if noticing how far God feels proves his nearness? What if seeing the space between God and us led to longing instead of despair? That's what I was able to share with Natalie.

I asked her if she owned a big pink Hummer. She clearly thought I was going way off topic and exasperatedly answered, "No."

I then proceeded to ask her a few hypothetical questions. "Imagine someone runs up to you, out of breath and deeply concerned, to tell you that your big pink Hummer was just stolen. What would your response be?"

She looked at me like it was the dumbest question she had ever been asked, but kindly played along. "I would tell them that I don't own a big pink Hummer," she replied.

"Would you be concerned or feel like you lost something that you once had?" I asked.

"No," she said, "I wouldn't care at all. I would just think they had me mistaken for someone else."

So far so good.

"Now," I continued with Natalie, "what is your most treasured and prized possession?"

She let the question sink in. I could tell she was taking this question quite seriously. I could see her mind's eye poring over every corner of her bedroom, closet, backpack, car, and locker. When her mind lighted upon the idea, I could see it in her eyes.

"I have a birthstone," she began. "My mom gave it to me." She hesitated, then said, "I live with my grandparents now." I could get the rest of the story from context. This stone was the only memento she had left to remember her late mother. "I keep the birthstone in a wooden box on my dresser. Every morning when I wake up, I open the box, take out my birthstone, and hold it for a few seconds before putting it back and closing the lid."

I wish you could have seen the sparkle in her eyes as she described her greatest treasure. It was almost as if I could see the stone she was describing just by looking at the marvel it held in her eyes.

"Now," I continued more slowly, "what would happen if that same person came up to you and told you the birthstone from the box on your dresser was missing?"

The hypothetical thought alone must have made her heart icy and her once shining eyes cold.

"I would be devastated," she confessed.

I pressed the point, "Why would you be devastated over the birthstone but not over the big pink Hummer?"

Natalie looked as if I had asked her why she would be devastated if her unicorn went missing instead of one of her grandparents. "Because I actually have my birthstone. I would never even want a Hummer."

I smiled just a little bit and said softly, "Then why are you so surprised that you are devastated over feeling God's absence?"

The way her eyes lit back up immediately told me she understood my point.

God felt absent because he is real. Natalie couldn't have felt the absence of the big pink Hummer because she never had the big pink Hummer. However, she could easily understand what it would feel like to lose her birthstone because she once had and treasured her birthstone.

Using this example, Natalie was able to see that she couldn't feel devastated by God's absence unless she had once treasured his presence. Instead of her feelings of distance and loss being clues to God's nonexistence, these became foundations upon which she could prove to herself that God not only exists, but exists in relation to her specifically.

Natalie was able to see that when something treasured is lost, the longing for the lost treasure makes it impossible to say you never possessed it in the first place. There was a supreme groaning of loss, anger, and fear in Natalie's soul because her supreme treasure was not in the place she had found it before. God felt absent because God was once present.

Absence Proves Presence

Absence isn't the same thing as nonexistence. Something that does not exist cannot be absent, since it was never present to begin with.

And here's a key to the relationship between absence and presence: the more profound the presence, the more painful the absence. The heavier foot leaves a deeper track. The weight of God's presence leaves footprints on the soft soil of hearts that belong to him.

Therefore, if God is feeling absent in your life, let this be an encouragement to you that he very much exists and can very much be found. Perhaps the deep tracks left by God that feel like absence are really meant to be a trail we are to follow in order to find his presence once again.

As Samuel Rutherford, the powerful seventeenth-century preacher, put it, "I think the sense of our wants, when withal we have a restlessness and a sort of spiritual impatience under them . . . is that which maketh an open door for Christ: and when we think we are going backward, because we feel deadness, we are going forward; for the more sense the more life, and no sense argueth no life."[1]

After all, the desires we have are placed in our hearts for a reason. We hunger because there is food. We thirst because there is water. We feel God's absence because he truly exists and we are designed to be near him. Only God can satisfy our longings for God.

As C. S. Lewis famously put it, "If I find in myself a desire which no experience in this world can satisfy, the most probable explanation is that I was made for another world."[2] Feeling God's absence is not cause for shame and doubt but cause for pursuit.

Tracking Down Our Absent God

This is not a self-help book. You will not find "The Ten Steps to Feeling God's Presence" in these pages because such steps don't exist. This is also not a book about fighting off absence in order to get presence. Instead, between these covers you will find out how to understand absence. By changing your understanding of God's absence, many things in your life will change as a consequence.

You will finally figure out how God can be everywhere at once and yet extremely far. You will see why it is that the more of God you get, the more of God you want. You will learn what it means to search for an invisible and absent God. You will place this gap of thousands of years between Jesus' first coming and his second coming in its proper light. You will come to grips with why it is good news that God is present in suffering. You will discover what God may be up to in your life if you are experiencing a dark night of the soul.

Experiencing the presence of God here and now will not be served up on a silver platter at the end of this book. I fear that such an endeavor would defame the glory of God and claim that I—a sinful, earthly author—am able to put a leash around the Almighty. Since such an impossible and ill-guided search is not the intent of this book, I want to invite you deeper into God's absence. I want to beckon you to step more fully into what you do not know.

God is hiding in absence. God is waiting in darkness. God uses distance for good purposes. No matter where you are on the spectrum of experiencing God's presence and absence, you desperately need to grapple with this topic. Whether God feels incredibly close or hopelessly far, a fuller experience of God's absence will reveal mysteries to you that you didn't even know existed. Welcome to the inevitable and impossible search for our absent God.

TWO

TRASH BAG COVERED WALLS

Why does God have to be absent?

> *The creation was subjected to futility, not*
> *willingly, but because of him who subjected it.*
> —ROMANS 8:20

The first time I experienced God's absence was actually one of the most profound experiences of his presence I've ever had. I remember the setting of that moment clearly. The walls of the tiny room corralling my fellow sixth graders and me were covered with thick black trash bags. A few muted red stage lights made the room feel like a mystic cave partially lit by two rubies. Artificial smoke spewed from the front-right corner of the room in rhythm with a faint hissing sound. The room was hot.

We had just finished two hours of recreation under a triple-digit Oklahoma sun, and the Hefty bags did little to improve the room's already anemic ventilation. Above the door leading into the room was a huge wooden sign with the words *Red 2* written in what looked like bloody war paint. We were like the enslaved Hebrews from the book of Exodus entering through the crimson-soaked doors of our homes before the angel of death made its way through the camps of Egypt. This was my very first youth camp.

The students were split up by grades. Each grade was assigned a color, and each color was broken into different groups and given a number. The sixth grade was assigned the color red, and I was drafted into group two. Every group was given their own room in which they met, sang songs, and received announcements and instructions. But these were not felt-board, Bible-poster, Sunday school classrooms. These rooms were decked out in a wide range of themes. I don't remember Red 2's theme, but I do remember the trash bags on the walls and one particularly warm evening of worship.

The Hefty sacks provided a cheap and quick solution to cover up whatever droll wallpaper or distracting signage hung on the walls before the camp began. The strategy was successful. The room was dark and insular. It wasn't creepy, but it did feel secluded. The red lights and fog machine added to the reflective ambience and made us eager sixth-graders feel as if we were in on something forbidden and foreboding.

As we funneled into the room and took our spots in the many rows of chairs, music began to play from somewhere between the room's two ruby-red eyes of gel-screened lights, about six or seven feet away from the fog machine, hissing like a snake in the corner. Over the fog machine, the band began to play a song we were all familiar with. The tune had been taking over radio time in cars and stage time in churches for months now. It had become a sort of anthem for the camp, and especially for Red 2. The opening notes of the song began, and the plastic, cavernous room seemed to swallow me up and I experienced one of my young life's most profound moments of reflection.

MercyMe's "I Can Only Imagine" began. I remember being overcome with the idea of standing in the presence of God. I closed my eyes and pictured what it would be like to stand before God face-to-face. Just chubby, awkward, sixth-grade David in his puka shell necklace, standing before the Almighty. David before God. Mortal before divine.

What would I do? I didn't know. What would it be like? I couldn't even imagine. My eyes filled with tears and my young heart found a surprising new hunger. I wanted to see God. I wanted to be in his presence. Ache filled me as I hurt with this new desire. I didn't want to feel God, I wanted to behold him. I wanted to see him with my own eyes, just as he is. This moment of worship was fantastic, but it wasn't good enough. I wanted God. No substitutes. No mediators. Not one inch of space between him and me. I wanted to be in the presence of the one and only God.

When I opened my eyes to the ruby lights, hissing fog, and Hefty bags, I didn't see God; I only saw a bunch of other sixth graders in their chairs. Disappointment flooded my heart. I wanted to do more than just "imagine" being with God. I wanted to be with God. But the thick, dark plastic seemed to choke out the possibility. The black trash bags weren't just covering the walls; they were forming a blockade, keeping my body trapped in the room with all the heat and sweat brought in from our recreation.

My skin seemed to be made out of the stuff as well. Plastic skin, holding my soul within my flesh like the plastic wallpaper, was holding my body within the room. I wanted to shred them both. Peel off skin and undress walls until I was out of this world and in the presence of God. But there was space between God and me. How could a desire so deep have been awakened and a moment so rich have been lived, only to open my eyes to the same world I left when I shut them?

Unfortunately, neither the bags nor the heavens were ripped open during the last few days of church camp. Neither have they torn open for me at any of the camps, conferences, church services, late-night prayer sessions, multiday fasts, or exquisite worship experiences I've been a part of ever since.

Maybe you have had an experience like this as well. You have closed your eyes in rapturous wonder at the majesty of God, only to open them again to your old habitat of absence. What is the one experience in your life that has opened you up to the presence of God the most? What was the room like? What sounds were there? Was it a song, a sermon, a poem, or a view that broke your heart open like the thin skin of a water balloon? What did you feel after the moment was over? How long did the moment stick with you? Many of us have had these moments of presence, only to be left with spans of absence.

I had a moment within those trash bag covered walls that set a fire in my heart that no experience on this earth has been able to quench. I wanted to be in God's immediate presence. But that presence has been blocked by the plastic barrier of this flesh and this world. God was absent to me in the way I most desired him to be present. God was absent in the way I most desired because his full and immediate presence was not before me. But that does not mean that God was not present with me at all. He was present with me in the way I most needed in that moment.

This is the truth of absence and presence that every single person lives and wrestles with: God is absent in the way we most desire, but present in the way we most require.

Desired Presence. Required Presence.

That really is the shortest way to sum up the meaning of this book, so I will say it again for good measure: God is absent in the way we most desire, but present in the way we most require. But this truth demands that we understand something right away. God can be present in more ways than one, and God can be absent in more ways than one. What kind of presence are we talking about when we say that God is absent in the way we most desire? What mode of God's presence do we desire most?

The answer is simple. We most desire God's actual presence.[1] God's actual presence is the face-to-face, unencumbered, completely revealed and unmediated form of his presence. This is the presence the Bible promises to those who believe in Jesus. The promise speaks of a day when we will live with God and be his people. This type of God's presence has been his plan and promise throughout all time.[2] This is not to say that the other ways in which God is present are fake or fraudulent, only lesser by degree. So when I talk about the presence we most desire or the absence we most profoundly experience, I am usually referring to God's actual nearness. Actual presence is presence desired.

But what do I mean when I say that God is present in the way we most require? In what ways can God be present that are separate from the ways in which he is absent? God is present with us in three ways: generally, relationally, and visually.

His general presence refers to his omnipresence. God is present everywhere by necessity, so he is generally present. His relational presence refers to how he is present to a Christian in a way in which he is absent to a non-Christian. God enters into a covenant of closeness with those who have been reborn in Christ and lives inside of them through his Holy Spirit. That is a radical kind of presence and one that is required to live the Christian life.

Finally, God can be present visually. This one is rare, even for Christians. This type of presence refers to seeing God with your eyes, hearing God with your ears, or experiencing him with one of your senses in a way that renders void all attempts to explain it away.

Each of these three forms of God's nearness is presence required. They are required because God must be present for us to be saved. God must act for us to react. So God reveals himself either generally, relationally, or visually in order to bring about the salvation we require.

As we move forward, please keep these categories in mind. Whether you believe in God or not, your strongest desire is to see God as he actually is in Christ.[3] In fact, the promised end of each and every Christian is not only to see Jesus as he truly is, but also to become like him. However, we do not yet see him in this way. Therefore, God is present to us in the ways we most require: his general presence, his relational presence, and his visual presence.

First John 3:2 says this beautifully: "Dear friends, now we are children of God, and what we will be has not yet been made known. But we know that when Christ appears, we shall be like him, for we shall see him as he is" (NIV).

One of the clearest places to see the separation between the presence we most desire and the presence we most require is in the moment in which they were severed. In the beginning of the Bible, the book of Genesis records the moment in which presence desired was separated from presence required.

The Fall

The absence of God has been experienced by every human being since Adam and Eve were expelled from the garden of Eden. It could even be said that no one has felt God's absence more deeply than Adam and Eve because no one has experienced the presence of God more fully than they did. The first man and woman enjoyed the pre-fall presence of God. They most fully experienced what it is like to be separated from God's full and immediate presence because they experienced God's presence in a way no other living human has. Before the fall, the walls of their lives had not yet been barricaded with black trash bags. Humans could be present with God.

But presence did not persist. Sin came between God and man when Adam and Eve rebelled against the Lord's good and perfect command. God gave the first couple liberty to eat all that the garden had to offer. There was only one tree out of the multitudes from which they were not to eat, and as we all have, Adam and Eve broke the law of God. This story is a familiar one to many people, but I want to look at it through the lens of God's presence and absence.

Right after eating the forbidden fruit, Genesis 3:8 says that Adam and Eve "heard the sound of the LORD God walking in the garden in the cool of the day" (NASB). What a dramatic statement of presence. God was walking. The Creator of legs was going for a stroll. The Inventor of days was enjoying the coolness of one. God was present in the garden. Leaves were shuffling under his footfall. Branches were bending as he walked by and springing back into place as he passed.

But God doesn't have a body and is not confined to space. Bible scholars explain that the God who walked in the garden of Eden was God the Son, who would later be called Jesus.[4] In the beginning, God lived with man. That's how the story of our world began, and it is how the story of our world will end—God living with us in the person of Jesus.

That is actual presence. God could be heard in the garden. That is the kind of interaction I wanted to have in Red 2's cave of worship. I wanted God to be so near that I could hear chair legs scratching the floor as he moved everything out of the way to get to me. This is the kind of presence your heart most longs for. But as Adam and Eve heard the crunching leaves and whipping branches of God drawing near, it was not desire that overtook them, but dread.

In Genesis 3:8, after hearing the sound of God's presence moving in the garden, we are struck with a profound statement of absence: "The man and his wife hid themselves from the presence of the LORD God." They hid from God. They sought out protection from his presence. When God's feet were heard in the leaves, they jumped in the bushes. Why?

Bad Things Hide When Good Things Arrive

As children, when we did something wrong, we often tried to hide. We either tried to conceal the evidence of our wrongdoing or hide ourselves from the parental wrath soon to come. Adam and Eve found themselves in the same situation. Confronted with God's impending presence, they hid themselves from God.

Absence is not always or exclusively an action of God. Adam and Eve jumped into the bushes. In their sin, they wanted to be far from God. They preferred absence to presence. They pushed God away because of his holiness and their sin. This will forever be the response of sinful man to a holy God. Even if an unholy sinner could enter heaven, as theologian J. C. Ryle has said, "His only desire would be to be cast out!"

Instinctively, they knew the presence of their evil could not be in the presence of God's goodness. They wanted to hide what they had done and what they had become. When confronted with goodness, that which is bad seeks a hiding place, whether behind bushes or lies. Bad things hide when good things arrive.

But hiding in the bushes could not provide sufficient distance between God's presence and man's sin. Adam and Eve hid, but not well enough. They didn't know their absence was about to get far worse. No bush was big enough to put enough space between God and them. Complete separation from God was what their sin had earned them. Divine Absence entered the world. Humans and God were no longer present with each other. Nearness gave way to distance. Adam and Eve were separated from their creator. Absence became their new address. And to this day we have never moved out.[5]

You may have picked up this book because the title resonated with you. You saw the words *When God Isn't There* and immediately connected with them because you've felt this way about God. You are not alone and you are not crazy. Nearly every person I've ever met has felt this way. Feeling like God isn't there is not a delusion but a reality.

We have lost our connection with God. The sin of Adam and Eve created absence from the type of God's presence we most desire— his actual presence. We feel this fracture no matter how much our relationship with God grows. It doesn't matter how deep we drop the bucket of our faith into God's well, we never seem to be able to pull up a full pail. Because of sin, we ended up with a God who isn't there.

However, you may not have picked up this book solely because you wanted answers to why God felt far to you. You may also be haunted by the question, *If God is so good, why does he feel so far?* I've asked the same question myself. Why do my bad sins make a good God absent?

What Absence Says About God

Growing up in church, I quickly learned how to share my faith. There was this tract everyone in my church used called "The Roman Road." By using verses from the book of Romans, the little blue pamphlet walked non-Christians along a path from thinking that they were pretty good people, all the way to confessing their sins at the foot of the cross. But there was one pothole for me in "The Roman Road."

The strategy of the tract was to help people see themselves as sinners. The first signpost on the road was Romans 3:23, which says, "For all have sinned and fall short of the glory of God" (NIV). The verse was strengthened by a string of questions: Have you ever done anything wrong? Have you told a lie, cheated on a test, stolen a candy bar? Eventually most people admitted they had done something wrong.

The next mile marker along the Roman road explained that our sin separates us from God. The candy bar we stole put a gap between us and the Almighty. The gap is so cavernous and wide that we could never cross it. We are destined to be separated from God forever because of our sin.

This is what I couldn't understand. How can a candy bar create a crevice and a piece of fruit condemn the entire world? If God is all about forgiveness, why can't he just let it go? If God is all powerful, why is sin such an obstacle? If God's presence was in God's plan, how could absence have snuck in? Even into the later years of my faith, I struggled with the mechanics of how sin actually removed me from God—and what that said about God for letting it happen.

If we aren't careful, questions like these lead us to form false pictures of what God is like. Two common false pictures of God are God as a bully and sin as Kryptonite.

The Bully

What I loved about playing on the playground at school was that all the games were made up. There wasn't a list of rules printed on the underside of the monkey bars or a scoreboard keeping tabs next to the seesaws. We got to make up our own rules. That is, until the bully showed up. We've all had bullies in our lives. And of course the natural habitat of the bully is the schoolyard playground.

The bully makes his own rules, and they apply as martial law to everyone within his jurisdiction. When the other kids don't play by his rules, the bully claims entire areas of the playground for himself. "If you don't play my way, then you can't play here at all." The ways of the bully are absolute. If you don't want to play dodge ball where headshots count, then you aren't allowed on the asphalt. If you don't want to play basketball where no fouls are called, then you aren't allowed on the court. If you don't do things the bully's way, then you don't get to play.

This is how many of us view our separation from God. If we don't play by his rules, we don't get to play at all. We think of the garden as God's playground. Surely it was because Adam and Eve didn't play by God's rules in the garden that he kicked them out. Like some kind of vindictive meanie, God pushes people away who don't do things the way he likes. Absence is the product of strict rules enforced by hurt feelings. This is the first false view of absence we can fall into.

Kryptonite

Superman was one of the first superheroes to be created. In April 1938, the Man of Steel debuted in Detective Comics (now better known as DC). The world was infatuated with this godlike hero of virtue from the planet Krypton. But, since this was one of the comic book world's first great heroes, neither the public nor the writers knew that good superhero stories need compelling superhero weaknesses.

In order to keep writing good stories about Superman's clashes with evil and his struggle for good, the possibility of defeat needed to exist. But Superman had no weakness. The booming franchise was on the brink of running aground. The stories were getting boring due to a lack of true and compelling conflict. That is, until the writers of the radio program, *The Adventures of Superman*, took it upon themselves to solve the problem.

Five years after Superman made his first appearance on earth, Kryptonite came down from the heavens. Kryptonite drained Superman of his powers. He could not exist along with Kryptonite. This glowing green rock from Superman's home planet was able to do what nothing else could—weaken the Man of Steel. Superman was now a printing press of great stories driven by greater conflict.

My struggle with understanding why our sin has to separate us from God was that it made God into Superman and sin into Kryptonite. Sure, Superman was strong, but he could not exist along with Kryptonite. In the same way, we think God is powerful, but he has a weakness: sin. We think God cannot be present where sin is because he is weak against it. If sin separates us from God, we decide it must have a power over him that he cannot conquer. We believe God flees from the power of sin, creating our separation, so absence is seen as the product of a powerful God repelled by a powerful force.

Not only did understanding sin in this way confuse my conception of God, it made me question the storyline of the Bible itself. Sin that could separate us from an almighty God seemed to be too convenient of an explanation. It was the comet of Kryptonite dropping in from the sky. Furthermore, it made God weak. Could God really not overcome sin? There had to be a better explanation for why sin separated me from my God.

Electrical Outlet Caps

Every time I look at an electrical outlet with one of those child-safe caps on it, I think of my buddy Drew. When he was four years old, Drew did the one thing a child is not supposed to do with a power outlet. He was hanging out at the church where his dad was a youth minister. Drew's dad was in his office, and Drew was entertaining himself in the youth room with his dad's ring of keys jingling in his hand. On the key ring was a tiny replica crucifixion nail. Drew held the nail in his hand and made his way to a power outlet. He took the replica crucifixion nail and jammed it into one of the youth room's power sockets.

The power in the entire building zapped off. The breakers clapped. But somehow, despite all logic, Drew wasn't harmed at all. It was a miracle. Nevertheless, you can bet his parents put those safety caps on every outlet in the youth room and their house from then on.

Outlets are not bad. They are fantastic. I use them to hook up my toaster, my Xbox, and my wife's essential oil diffuser (okay, I like how it smells too). However, something as powerful as electricity must be treated with respect. You have to use it according to its own rules and standards.

There is not a physical rule book that everyone who encounters electricity is given. As we grow up, we learn how to relate and how not to relate to electricity. But little children like Drew do not yet understand the power of electricity or how to properly relate to it. So their parents, in love, install plastic outlet covers to protect their children from harm. They put separation between the electricity and the child for the child's own sake.

God is like electricity. He is powerful, unique, and therefore demands respect. By his very nature, there are ways we can and cannot relate to him. He has pure, good, and perfect qualities that make up the uniqueness of who he is. This is known as his holiness. We must relate to God in ways consistent with his character or the results will be detrimental. Putting sin in the presence of God would be like putting a nail in the holes of an electrical outlet. The flesh of sinful man cannot survive an encounter with the power and glory of God. Sin does not mix with God.[6]

That is why God creates absence. He separates the electricity of his holiness from the flesh of our sin. This is for our protection. The absence of God is the little plastic outlet cover. God puts distance between him and us for our own good. His absence is grace.

The Grace of Absence

Grace is undeserved kindness.[7] It is hard for us to think about our separation from God as a kindness, but it is. Since sin cannot survive an encounter with holiness, just as Drew shouldn't have survived his encounter with electricity, what would happen if holiness drew near to sin? What would happen if a holy God came close to sinful man? If both cannot be in the same space, one would have to stop existing if the space were ever shared. Man would be destroyed by God.

Understanding absence as the plastic outlet cap helps us debunk our false views of God as the bully on a playground or Superman fleeing from Kryptonite. God does not arbitrarily come up with rules and standards on a whim like some bully making up rules to a game only he wants to play. God himself is the standard. His holiness sets the rules. We are not thrown out of his presence because we didn't play the game right. We are separated from him in grace so that we may not be destroyed. Yes, separation is a punishment, and we don't want to experience it forever, but it is also part of God's plan for presence.

In the same way, sin is not Kryptonite to God. Sin is not an outside force pushing God away. It is a substance utterly distinct and separate from him. The essence of who God is in his holiness makes this distinction. Separation is not a reaction to protect God; it is a chosen response to protect us. Sin does not hold power over God like Kryptonite does over Superman. God does not run in fear or repulsion from sin. Instead, God places space between himself and sinful humanity so that we may not be consumed. Consider these verses from Isaiah:

> Behold, the LORD's hand is not shortened, that it cannot save,
>   or his ear dull, that it cannot hear;
> but your iniquities have made a separation
>   between you and your God,
> and your sins have hidden his face from you
>   so that he does not hear. (59:1–2)

We are separated from God. His face is hidden from us. All this is a result of our sin. Without God's holiness there is no sin; without God's grace there is no absence. We are absent from God because of our sin and his holiness. God is absent from us because of his grace and our guilt. Absence is our fault. We are the sinners. And for us, this was a tremendous loss.

Paradise Lost

In J. R. R. Tolkien's famous trilogy, The Lord of the Rings, Gimli the dwarf has a beautiful and haunting moment. Gimli is a hard-nosed, stubborn, ill-countenanced grump whose people are not too fond of elves. Gimli's mood changes, however, when he and his travel companions find themselves in the enchanted woods of Lothlórien.

This forest of legendary elves has a magical quality that can be seen in every leaf and twig. After spending a great deal of time in the enchanted woods, meeting the fair queen Galadriel, and hearing the sweet music sung by the people of the treetops, the dwarf and his companions depart from Lothlórien. Gimli grows terribly sad as he reflects on his time there.

"I have looked the last upon that which was fairest." These are the words of Gimli recalling the beauty of Lothlórien. He continues, "Henceforward I will call nothing fair . . . I have taken my worst wound in this parting, even if I were to go this night straight to the Dark Lord."[8] Gimli has seen the fairest of all things in the world and knows nothing will be found to match it. All else will seem dark to him compared to the light of the woods he has left.

Eden was God's perfect creation. Inside that perfection, he met perfectly with Adam and Eve. We haven't been there, but God's general presence provides us with a faint memory of what no longer exists. We fear that Adam and Eve were the ones who looked last upon that which was fairest. Their absence screams in our hearts, begging for us all to return to the most desired presence of our God. Sin has caused our worst wound in separating us from God's actual presence.

All people seek to fill the void of God's absence with the presence of pleasure, success, or even religion. We look upon things that men call good and fair, but all things leave us feeling far from that which we most desire. Nothing is without the sting of absence. Nothing removes the dream of Eden from our minds. This is the great pain that all mankind lives with: the absence of God.

Wilderness Wear

In Eden, humans willingly severed their connection with God. At that point, God could have done away with us, abandoned us, or scrapped creation and started over. But in his grace, God used separation to preserve us and prepare us for his presence. In his kindness, he put plastic caps on the outlets of his glory. This grace and kindness is beautifully pictured in his sending Adam and Eve from the garden.

Adam and Eve broke God's law when they ate from the forbidden tree. Since God is always just, ascribing penalties to wrongdoing like a good judge, the two had to be punished. But the punishment that sin deserves is more severe than just getting booted out of Eden, though that was severe. Sin against the eternal God's eternal law earns an eternal punishment. A death that brings unending separation from God is the only correct sentence for all sin. But God did not immediately put Adam and Eve to death, nor did he overlook the punishment sin deserved. He punished them as his holiness required but showed grace to them as his love desired.

Adam and Eve were naked and felt ashamed about their sin. So God sacrificed some nearby animals and made clothes for them out of the skins (Gen. 3:21). This was a shadow of another sacrifice God would make in the future.[9] On the cross, God poured out all his punishment on Jesus, the perfect Lamb of God. This sacrifice not only took on the punishment we deserved but it clothes us so that we can be allowed to enter God's presence.[10]

If we were to come into the actual presence of God as naked, shameful, and sinful as Adam and Eve were, we would be struck dead. But when God gives us the wilderness wear of Jesus' sacrifice, we are clothed in a holy covering that allows us to not only enter the actual presence of God but to live in the actual presence of God as it was before the fall. In Jesus, the clothes for the guilty become the pathway back to Eden.

It is extremely appropriate that it was a crucifixion nail that stood between my friend Drew and the power surging within the electrical socket. Somehow he was able to have an extreme encounter with electricity and walk away unscathed. The nail from the crucifixion stood between him and the source of power, and miraculously his life was spared.

In the same way, it is Jesus on the cross that allows us to encounter God's powerful presence without being utterly destroyed. His crucifixion nails give us the only point of entry into the otherwise unendurable presence of God. The cross of Christ earns our way back into God's presence.

But we are not back in Eden yet. God is still absent. While on this earth, we still wear the flesh of our sin and cannot stand in God's actual presence.[11] But a day is coming when we will put on the new clothes of Christ and stand before God's presence like I so longed to do in the cave of Red 2.

THREE

GOD: ABSENT AND EVERYWHERE

Isn't God always present?

So Cain went out from the Lord's
presence and lived in the land of Nod.
—Genesis 4:16 (niv)

S anta was real in the Bowden house. Meticulous preparations were
always made by my mom and dad to ensure that every Christmas
morning was full of convincing proofs. Reindeer were clearly on the
roof the night before, because there were droppings that had rolled off
onto the lawn and hoof prints that could be examined by ladder (not
to mention I clearly heard them clopping about up there in the night).

Rudolph was Christmas Eve's whimsical jokester, as we came to
find out. He would always leave his calling card, a half-eaten carrot,
somewhere near one of our home's entry points. Whether it was
slid down the chimney, slipped through the doggy door, or left for
us in the mailbox with the flag up, Rudolph always had something
up his furry sleeves.

But it wasn't just the reindeer that left clues all over the place like clumsy criminals. Santa's handiwork was also clear to see. The cookies left on the fireplace were always 75 percent eaten. Enough to honor the quality of our baking but not gone entirely, so we wouldn't wonder if he had just tossed them in disgust down on unsuspecting Oklahoma City from atop his sleigh. The crumbs from the cookies were also integral to the retelling of the nighttime plot. They formed a breadcrumb trail for my sister and me to piece together every Christmas morning. Santa clearly started eating at the chimney, then headed to the den to drop off the presents.

One year it seemed we hadn't left enough milk out for him, so he helped himself to the carton in our fridge. If the crumbs didn't lead us to the fridge, then the note written in Santa's own script would have done the trick. Next to his newly dirtied glass, a small scrap of paper from our grocery list pad said, "Great cookies require great amounts of milk. Thanks.—S.C."

Santa was quite real to me as a child. But in retrospect, Santa was also kind of creepy. A costumed man skulking down our filthy chimney, tiptoeing through our family den, and rummaging about in our refrigerator is not normally seen as a welcomed guest. You would think the songs we sang about Santa would have tipped us off. "He sees you when you're sleeping. He knows when you're awake."

These traits should earn Santa not sainthood but a restraining order. Parents tell their children that they better be good because Santa is watching. If they don't clean behind their ears, they'll get a lump of coal in their stocking. Like some kind of holy Peeping Tom, Santa has become the behavior watchdog for many families. St. Nick is everywhere, and he's going to get you.

The only reason Santa needs to see everything is so he can reward or punish us. Santa's presence is all about our behavior. His rosy red cheeks grin in satisfaction when we are good boys and girls and frown in disappointment when we are naughty. The presence of Santa is all about presents.

When we think about God, some of us have similar thoughts. God is everywhere. He is always present, always watching. We view God like a watchful principal, ready to spank us with a ruler when we step out of line. Like Santa, we think God gives us gifts when we're good and a lump of coal when we're bad. But God is not present so that he can spy on us, marking his list with "Naughty" demerits and "Nice" golden star stickers. God is present everywhere because of his nature.

He is present everywhere because without his presence nothing would exist. So in order for us to properly talk about the ways in which God isn't there, we must first understand why God is there and what it means for God to be near. God isn't Santa, but he does see you when you're sleeping.

But Isn't God Everywhere?

The presence of God must frame all discussions about his absence. We cannot properly understand one without the other. Maybe you have seen one of those black-and-white pictures that look like a black goblet if you look at it one way and two white faces staring at each other if you look at it another way.

These optical illusions are in the category of "double meaning" images. Your perception of what the image contains is directly related to how you are looking at it. You didn't see the full picture that this "double meaning" optical illusion was trying to show you until you realized the existence of both images and saw them for yourself.

In the same way, the full picture of God contains the black goblet of his presence and the two white faces of his absence. The white faces on either side will not come into focus until we have a sharp understanding of what the black goblet of God's presence actually looks like. On the other hand, we must not allow the white faces of absence to overtake the clear borders placed around the black goblet of God's presence.

After all, "God accomplishes his promises, first and foremost, by becoming present."[1] Just as he rescued his people Israel out of the land of Egypt "with his own presence," so he brings us out of the land of sin and death with his nearness and intervention.[2] Each must have its own place. We can't really understand how amazing God's relational presence is with all Christians unless we first understand the limits of his general presence with all humanity. We must allow presence to define absence and absence to chasten our understanding of presence.

Absence is seen by noticing where the different aspects of God's presence (actual, visible, relational, and general) *are* and *are not*. As we begin to more fully understand what we believe about God's presence, we can more appropriately begin to allow God's absence to take shape. This is important because until we see the absence of God in proper relationship to his presence, we will not see the full image of what it means for God to be near or far. So let us first seek to understand what it means for God to be omnipresent with us.

First of all, we must figure out what we mean by omnipresence. Let's start by using an easier word. We will refer to the fact that God is present everywhere at the same time as God's "general presence." It is a common Christian belief that God is generally present. In fact, the most common view of general presence doesn't just say that God is present everywhere, but that God *must* be present everywhere. General presence is necessary. The general presence of God is necessary for three reasons: (1) his immensity, (2) his sustaining power, and (3) his sovereignty.

Immensity

Picture God as a vast and endless ocean and the entire created universe as a plastic Wiffle ball. Now imagine that the Wiffle ball is placed on the surface of the ocean and begins to sink until it is completely subsumed by the gargantuan body of water. The ocean is so titanic and filling, and the Wiffle ball is so small and porous, that the ocean completely fills the ball. In the same way, God's presence fills the universe as the ocean would fill the Wiffle ball. The ocean is present elsewhere, too, though the Wiffle ball is not. God is so large that he fills absolutely everything. We would not say that the ocean is the Wiffle ball or the Wiffle ball is the ocean. Neither the identity of the ball or the ocean is lost, but one is swallowed by the other.

God could never create a place larger than he could fill. Looking for a place where God is not is as futile as looking for the edge of the world. There is no part, in all the created universes, in which God is not found. And for Christians who not only live in God's general presence, but in his relational presence, too, the words of Deuteronomy 33:12 bring beautiful assurances to the truth of God's immensity: "The beloved of the LORD dwells in safety. The High God surrounds him all day long, and dwells between his shoulders."

Sustaining Power

Another principle of God's general presence is his sustaining power. It's not as if God is simply watching the happenings of the world the same way you and I watch a movie. He doesn't just pop in every so often to turn up the volume or change the disc. God himself is the director of every actor and actress. He's the designer of every set piece and camera shot. He's the composer of every note in the score and every letter in the dialogue.

Hebrews 1:3 tells us that Jesus sustains the universe by his "powerful word" (NIV). Colossians 1:17 explains that, not only were all things created through Jesus, but all things are continually held together by him. If God were absent from any place in all of creation for a single moment, creation itself would cease to exist. Therefore, God must be everywhere, sustaining and upholding the world. Creation's existence depends on the presence of its Creator.

Sovereignty

Third, God is generally present as a result of his omniscience and omnipotence. *Omniscience* is the word we use to communicate that God is all-knowing. God knows everything that goes on in his creation and everything that will go on in his creation. God knows everything from who will be elected Prime Minister of England to who will fall in love in the state of Kansas.

God is also omnipotent. This means that God is all-powerful. There is nothing in all of creation that his might would fail to accomplish. Anything God sets his mind to do, his arm will achieve. Therefore, since the Bible declares God to be all-knowing and all-powerful, his general presence is necessary. God must be present in all places at all times to do all things.

Perhaps the psalmist David most clearly explained these three ideas in Psalm 139:7–10.

> *Where shall I go from your Spirit?*
> *Or where shall I flee from your presence?*
> *If I ascend to heaven, you are there!*

If I make my bed in Sheol, you are there!
If I take the wings of the morning
    and dwell in the uttermost parts of the sea,
even there your hand shall lead me,
    and your right hand shall hold me.

Let me say this very clearly: God is never fully absent. God is always there. The teachings of the Bible demand God's unceasing, universal general presence. There is nowhere you can go, nowhere you can hide, and nowhere you can fall where God's general presence is absent. In the entire earth, in the fullness of the cosmos, and even outside the fabric of creation, God is fully present in his general, omnipresent nature. Nothing in this book will contradict that fact. God's general presence is never absent.

God's general presence is required for the world to exist. But his general presence is not the presence we most desire. General presence is not actual, face-to-face presence. It is not visible, see-with-your-eyes presence. It is not relational, access-through-Jesus presence. General presence is presence required, not presence desired. We must draw firm lines around the black goblet of God's general presence. While he is absent in the way we most desire, God is always present in the way we most require.

If God Is Everywhere, Why Does He Still Feel Absent?

I realize the topic of God's presence and absence can be frustrating, even tiresome, to wrap your head around. And even though Scripture tells us that God is never fully absent, I'm betting you still have unanswered questions. In fact, they may be the very questions that drove you to take up reading this book in the first place. They're probably the same kind of questions that drove me to write this book. Questions like:

> If I am in a relationship with God, why does he feel so absent?
> If I am supposed to be God's daughter (or son), why does he feel like a distant father?
> If the Holy Spirit is dwelling in me now that I'm a Christian, why do I not feel that different from before I believed?
> How can God always be present with me if he feels so absent?

You are not alone in asking these questions. Christians all over the world and all through the years have struggled with these and more difficult questions regarding the distance between God and us. Maybe doubt is beginning to creep into your faith. Resentment may be filling your prayers and thoughts. Anger and desperation may overtake you when you stare at the stars and scream out for a sign.

You may just have a little stinging suspicion in the back of your mind that God may not be as close at hand as you once thought. Now that you are maturing in your faith, you are beginning to see problem areas and wondering where God is. Whatever you are going through, I hope that what I am about to explain to you will help a great deal.

The Desire for Presence

While it's true that God is everywhere, God's general presence awakens a desire in us that it does not fulfill. We want to be in relationship with God, behold God, and be with God. We desire more than the general presence of God. But how, you ask, can God be absent in any real sense if he is always present in some way?

Think of it like this: Imagine you are at a coffee shop. You're sitting in the back corner with a fresh cup. There are other people in the café, but none of them are sitting at your table. So in that moment, everyone in the coffee shop is generally present with one another. But if a friend comes into the shop, walks up to you, and asks, "Is anyone with you?" you would answer, "No." You are generally present with others, but not in a uniquely relational way. Such is the general presence of God. He's always in the café, but that doesn't mean we're at the table with him.[3]

The general presence of God creates a general knowledge of God. Just as you would be generally aware of other people in the café, all humans are generally aware of God. Romans 1:19–20 says, "For what can be known about God is plain to them [all mankind], because God has shown it to them. For his invisible attributes, namely, his eternal power and divine nature, have been clearly perceived, ever since the creation of the world, in the things that have been made." God can be clearly seen in nature, morality, and in the essence of who we are as human beings. On top of every mountain, in the tugging of your inner conscience, and in all humanity's inclination that they were made for something more, God has made himself known.

It's like when I smell bacon. I don't care if I'm not that hungry, if it isn't breakfast time, or if I already had bacon today. If I smell bacon, I will not be satisfied until I have some bacon. This is because my senses have become aware that bacon is nearby. But just because I can smell bacon does not mean I have the bacon in my hand or on my tongue. Therefore, the general presence of the bacon's aroma has awakened a desire that it cannot fulfill. Smelling more bacon will not satisfy my stomach. Even if I knew the bacon was meant for me (if it were relationally present), I would still not be satisfied. The visible presence of bacon would only further excite my desire to eat the bacon. The only form of presence that would satisfy my desire is the actual presence of the bacon. The only thing that will satisfy the desire that the aroma has awakened is a full plate of bacon right in front of me and ready to be consumed.

The whole world is full of the aroma of God, and it's making everyone hungry. Everyone longs to *know* that which they are only *aware* of. God's presence fills this world, but only as an aroma, a hint, an awareness. This puts a rumble in the gut and an insatiability on the lips of every living thing. We hunger to know the God of whom we are only aware. Therefore, God's general presence creates an unfulfilled longing that makes us want to taste what we can only smell. God's presence creates absence.

We all feel the absence of God. The aroma of the meal we most long to consume is stuck in our nostrils, and it's only making us hungrier. Our desire for God is fueled by the overwhelming hints of his presence we see and feel throughout his world. Our bellies ache to be near the one we are so far from. Our stomachs groan to be with him instead of apart from him. Our mouths water for God. We desire to sit at his table and feast on all of him. But we're often stuck with grumbling guts, sitting in the café, waiting for God to come join our table.

God was generally present in the Red 2 room with me the night I sang "I Can Only Imagine," but the black trash bags of this world made his actual presence absent. He drew near to me in one sense, to show me his glory and give me the gift of his presence. But he also remained far off, to preserve my life and allure me to himself. I could smell the aroma of God in that room, but I could not partake of the feast.

If you feel this grumbling, remember that it is the aroma that causes the hunger. Have you ever said, "I'm not hungry," but then you smell food and instantly change your mind? It is the presence of food that makes us realize its absence in our stomachs. It is God's nearness that makes us notice his distance. The white faces of absence actually point out the black goblet of presence. God's absence is a product of his presence. So do not be discouraged when God feels far. I know that it hurts, as real hunger pangs do, but you have not been abandoned. There is a banquet of God's presence waiting for you.

The Bread of Life

Much like us, there were people in Jesus' day who hungered for more of what God had promised. After Jesus fed more than five thousand people with only two loaves of bread and five fish, the massive crowd followed him across the sea. They wanted him to provide them with their next meal. The mob was hungry, and they wanted Jesus to feed them. But Jesus did not perform another miracle.

Instead, he said something extremely unexpected: "I am the bread of life" (John 6:35). Jesus was saying that he is the meal for which the people truly hungered. Bread would not satisfy them, but Jesus would. The crowd didn't like this answer. They wanted to be fed immediately. So they left Jesus in droves. When Jesus offered his presence, the crowds responded with their absence.

Jesus has made the same promise to us. We are hungry. We are starving—some of us physically and some of us spiritually. And Jesus tells us that he is the meal for which we are so famished. He is the living Water that will once and for all quench our thirst. The relational presence offered through a relationship with Jesus is what we most require while on this earth and the only thing we need when we leave it.

However, there is a deeper satisfaction in Christ that we look forward to. There is a richer meal that awaits us in the actual presence of Jesus. A feast is promised to us when Jesus returns in all the glory of his actual presence. This banquet is called "The Marriage Supper of the Lamb." It is described in Revelation 19:6–9:

"Hallelujah!
For the Lord our God
    the Almighty reigns.
Let us rejoice and exult
    and give him the glory,
for the marriage of the Lamb has come,
    and his Bride has made herself ready;
it was granted her to clothe herself
    with fine linen, bright and pure"—

for the fine linen is the righteous deeds of the saints.

And the angel said to me, "Write this: Blessed are those who are invited to the marriage supper of the Lamb."

There will come a day when we will come to our Lord as a bride comes to her husband. Not one shred of intimacy will be missing from our union. Presence will be our chapel and our vows, our honeymoon and our homecoming. And there will be a meal in which all our cravings will be satisfied. At this feast, all our hungers will be filled, all our longings will be met. The God who filled our nostrils will be standing in front of our eyes.

We need only to respond to the Bread of Life. We need only make ourselves present with his promise of presence through Jesus. Don't make yourself absent to the offer of presence. For though we wait in absence, we wait patiently, joyously, and with hope because we know our absence is a product of presence.

God is everywhere, filling us like a Wiffle ball in the ocean. Jesus is the Bread of Life that sustains us while we sojourn through this world. He is unrelentingly near, which makes him feel unendingly far. So we wait. We wait in the ocean of presence for our absent God.

CHASING OUR ABSENT GOD

A Life of Absence

The Christian life is a life of absence.

We believe in an invisible God
But wait for the return of his incarnate Son.

We've been given the Spirit, the indwelling one,
But his guarantee is for things that are yet to come.

We trust in promises that have all been won
But wait for their fulfillment when all completion is done.

Our story is
Begun, but not finished.
Our new selves we've
Become, but not to the fullest.
Our victory is
Inaugurated, but not finally set.

So we are the believers amid the
Already and the not yet.

We are already residents of a home,
but do not yet live on the right street.
We are already citizens of a kingdom
that is not yet complete.
We are already owners of a harvest
that has not yet been reaped.
We are already children of a king
whose face we've not yet been able to greet.

There is so much we already hold,
But it is the not yet that we seek.

For before we met Christ
We happily saw ourselves as earth's inhabitants.
But now we know we are not yet home,
So the Christian life is a life of absence.

But this distance wasn't created by accident.
For within it something miraculous can happen.

Since we want more of God than we currently can access
Our longing for him is stirred up in the process.

As absence increases
So grows our avidity.
As new gaps are found
So abounds our intensity.
As distance is uncovered

We quicken our pace.
As more longing is discovered
We bear down in the race.

Because all this space
Between us and God
Is not arbitrary or random.
Instead God uses these chasms
To point us to the second Adam.

For

If God had never been absent
We would have never known Christ or his cross.
So though our separation feels like the highest cost
Not knowing Jesus' sacrifice would be the only real loss.

But now we get to know God
As he first planned
And as he truly wants—
A God who wouldn't abandon his creation
But would save them through sacrificial action.

So praise be to our God
Who knew that distance
Would best reveal his glory
Before it even happened.

Praise be to our God that
The Christian life is really
A life of absence.

FOUR

THE MOSES PRINCIPLE:
MORE WANTS MORE

Why does God feel farther the closer I get?

> *One thing have I asked of the* LORD,
>   *that will I seek after:*
> *that I may dwell in the house of the* LORD
>   *all the days of my life,*
> *to gaze upon the beauty of the* LORD
>   *and to inquire in his temple.*
> —PSALM 27:4

Buzz Lightyear's gloves were far too big for him that night. My nephew, Mason, was covered from helmet to space boots in his new *Toy Story* costume and couldn't wait to show Uncle David all his cool new ranger moves. The outfit looked great on him, and hilarious. The three colored voice-command buttons were fixed to his chest like badges of honor. The antigravity belt tightly hugged at his waist. He was a pretty heroic-looking Buzz for a two-year-old.

But the gloves must have missed their original packaging. I'm not saying that the gloves weren't included. They were just about ten sizes too big. Nearly an extra foot of loose plastic hung off my nephew's hands. The small red button, which was meant to be affixed to the forearm for easy laser access, drooped off the edges of his fingers as his arms flailed about. The gloves, which were almost up to his shoulders, flapped around with his every gesture. His arms were like one of those tall tubular figures being blown up and around by a large fan outside car dealerships.

The sight was sidesplitting, and Mason loved the attention. He began running up to each family member individually, wriggling his loose gloves in their face, and giggling wildly as if he had just told a joke that he was all too proud of. Mason had discovered a game that didn't exist before. He loved it, and so did we.

After half an hour of crying with laughter over Lightyear's limp arms, the novelty began to wear off for the adults. But not for Mason. Two-year-olds have a penchant for milking any good pleasure. He continued to come up to me and my red face, sore from laughing, and flick the loose plastic gloves repeatedly at it.

Mason's laughter had now turned into an invitation instead of a response. But I did not receive the gesture. I said, "Mason, I'm tired." His laughter grew louder, like a passive-aggressive insistence that I wouldn't want to miss out on this fine occasion for rare jubilance. "More! More!" Mason shouted. I had heard these words many times before and, most likely, so have you.

Whether we were flying or wrestling, tickling or dancing, Mason always wanted more. When he discovered a new joy, he couldn't get enough of it. One time wasn't enough and neither were twenty. More always wanted more. But I, along with every other adult in the known universe, tire far more quickly of games than two-year-olds do.

When you throw them in the air, they want you to do it again. Tossing them higher doesn't satisfy them; it awakens a new desire to be thrown higher still. A little fling up and down will no longer suffice once the heights of your strength have been discovered. Neither would a little giggle from me do now that Mason knew the intensity of the full-out belly laugh his loose gloves could bring. When they see something good, children want more of it.

This is incredibly true of God's presence. The more we get of it, the more we want. When we draw near to God in worship one Sunday, we want to draw nearer to him in song the next. When we experience a deep moment of honest and intimate prayer, we long to reach that place once more. When God is seen more clearly in his creation, we climb mountains and stare at oceans until we see him in such a way again. The more we get of God, the more we want of God. More wants more.

As with any adult playing with a two-year-old, however, the supply of more reaches an end. It is not as if God grows tired of tossing us up into the air higher and higher until we stop yelling for more, but either we grow tired of looking or the world cannot bear up under the weight of our desires. The night Buzz Lightyear's gloves were far too big, Mason found that the room had exhausted its resources of laughter. His desires for fun exceeded the room's ability to provide it.

We are often like Mason, playing in an oversized costume. We stumble upon something wild, beautiful, and joyous about our relationship with God that we hadn't yet discovered, and we want more. Like my night in the plastic-bag cave with Red 2, I wanted more of God than that room could provide. I wanted to be where I could only imagine, but found myself where I had always been. I wanted more God, but only got trash bags.

There is a presence of God that is absent to us—his actual presence. We cry for more, and the world says, "I'm tired." We scream, "Again!" and the universe replies, "Not yet."

Or maybe you are more like the adults in the room with a ceaselessly playing Buzz Lightyear scuttling at your feet. You know there is more of God to be discovered, more joy to be found, and more adventures to be had, but you are tired. You've laughed with God; you've cried with God; you've trusted him and experienced him. But now you just feel tired of running.

You've opened your eyes one too many times to the sight of black plastic walls. The cries of "More!" and "Again!" coming from your heart are burdensome. You roll your eyes at them like you do with the two-year-old who won't stop begging you to toss him in the air. We want more, but we're tired of chasing it down.

The Moses Principle

Moses was like Mason. Moses always wanted more. I think we can safely say that few human beings have experienced God on this earth to the extent that Moses did. From meeting God in the burning bush, to parting the Red Sea, to watching manna fall from heaven, Moses saw much of God. In fact, after Israel's escape from slavery in Egypt, God made it clear that Moses was the bearer of a special privilege when it came to God's presence.

After leading the Israelite people to Mount Sinai through the Red Sea and away from Pharaoh's army, God met with Moses on top of the mountain in a thick cloud.[1] Strict rules were given before God descended upon the peak. These rules prohibited anyone from setting an inch of their person on even the foot of the mountain.[2] The penalty for such an action was death.

No one was to enter into this unique presence of God except Moses. Like one of those nightclubs with a line of people outside waiting to get in, God unfastened the rope from the stanchion and invited Moses into his presence. This was VIP territory.

The thick darkness of God scorched the top of the mountain like a consuming cloud. The people were terrified. But Moses entered in, and he spent time on the mountain with God. Moses experienced what it was like to behold a level and an intensity of the presence of God that you and I cannot even fathom. But the more of God he got, the more of God he wanted. Even on the mountain-top, more wants more.

Exodus 33 tells us a story about Moses that makes him sound like my little nephew Mason. God had finished giving Moses some instructions when Moses made a unique and audacious request. "Please show me your glory," Moses said (v. 18). What? Hadn't he seen enough? Had the glory of God not been made manifest to him in manifold ways? Was the staff-to-serpent trick not enough for Moses? What about when God defied nature to push the flat and flooded sea up like walls and dried up the perpetually soaked sea floor so that it was like concrete? Was that not enough glory for Moses to behold?

He entered into the cloud of thick darkness on top of Mount Sinai. He went into the places of God where no human being had ever been. He spoke with God like one human speaks with another. He moved from general presence to relational presence to visible presence. After all this, had he not seen enough of God's glory? Apparently Moses had not.

This is the Moses Principle: more wants more. The presence of God had tossed the soul of Moses high into the air, and he wanted to sail higher still. The nearness of God tickled the heart of Moses, and he wanted to laugh more deeply still. The more Moses got of

God, the more Moses wanted of God. The more we experience of God in this life, the more of God we will desire. That is the Moses Principle.

Absence: Curse or Clue?

You've probably had a time in your life when you got more of God and wanted even more. That elation of discovery and depth can deeply impact us. But you've probably also experienced times when you felt a great distance between you and God. Since we often interpret intimacy with God as a reward, like being permitted into VIP territory, we conversely interpret distance as a punishment.

Absence is always a curse, we think. However, your ability to sense absence may actually be a clue of your love for God. Absence isn't always a curse; sometimes it's a clue.

I travel for a living. As a consequence I am constantly forced to be absent from my wife. After returning from a trip she always has the same question for me: "Did you miss me?" She wants to know if I noticed her absence, if I longed for her presence, if the distance between us was in any way insufferable for me. Of course, I always answer, "I missed you like crazy!"

I answer this way because it's completely true. I miss my wife when I'm away from her because I love her very much. In fact, the more I have come to love her, the more I have come to miss her when we are absent from each other. If I didn't love her so much, I wouldn't miss her so much. If I didn't love her at all, I wouldn't miss her at all. That is why the question, Did you miss me? is an important one. It is synonymous with, Do you still love me?

The same is true of our relationship with God. The more we come to love God, the more we long to be present with him. The only problem is, like Moses, we find that we want more of God's presence than we have been given. Even if that presence is as extreme as meeting God in a mighty cloud and hearing his voice thunder from it. We want more of God's presence because we are in love with him. We long for our God like I long for my wife.

If God feels far, it might be his voice calling out to you through the absence, saying, *"See, you do love me."* Absence doesn't guarantee that you are a bad Christian. Distance doesn't have to mean that you are far from God in a sinful, relational, or punishing way. Sometimes distance is a result of sin, but you may just be realizing, while you travel far from him on this earth, that you miss him because you love him. Let your feelings of absence translate into affirmations of passion. Let your inclinations of distance turn into assurances of love.

Cleft of the Rock

Moses was in love with God. This love drove him to request more of God. God answered, "I will make all my goodness pass before you and will proclaim before you my name. . . . But . . . you cannot see my face, for man shall not see me and live" (Ex. 33:19–20). This is the fundamental cap on God's presence. Humans cannot see God's face and live. We cannot be in God's actual presence in these sinful, fleshly bodies.

That means no one who is alive has seen God as he truly is.[3] God's face is covered, like a plastic cap on an electrical outlet. There is an absence between us and God that exists so that we may continue existing. This is critically important. There is a form of God we long to see that would kill us if we saw it.

This is not because God is like Medusa, who turns all people to stone as soon as they look upon her. The reason for separation is our sin and God's holiness. The two cannot dwell together. Like a nail in a power outlet, the flesh of sinful man cannot connect with the unveiled face of God and live.

However, like any good parent playing with the child they love, God doesn't grow tired of Moses' Buzz-Lightyear–like request for "More!" He told Moses that he would allow him to see all of his goodness. God was going to give Moses more of God. This is great news!

God wants to give us more of himself. He wants to be more present with us. God wants to fulfill our most audacious requests for presence. Even though Moses had seen much, God was going to give him more. God honors the Moses Principle. More wants more. More gives more.

In order to accomplish this giving of more, God instructed Moses to stand in the cleft of a rock so that his field of vision would be limited and controlled. You can picture the cleft of the rock as a small split in a great rock. The thin line in the stone offered a sliver of light through which Moses could catch a glance, like looking through a narrow crack in a door. This wasn't because God didn't want to be present with Moses, nor because God didn't want Moses to be present with him. It was for Moses' sake that this distance was maintained.

We cannot see all of God, and yet that is the longing of our hearts. We scream out for "More," but more could kill us. Understand this: while you are on this earth, God will always feel absent to some degree. The Christian life is one of absence. This is not because God is distant, aloof, or does not desire a relationship with us. On the contrary, in God's kindness he wants to give us the desires of our hearts. So he places each of us in the cleft of the rock.

When we ask for God's presence, to see more of his glory, God will give us a sliver of light through which to behold him. We have this promise in Scripture: "Draw near to God, and he will draw near to you" (James 4:8). This drawing near may be a worship song, a moment in nature, a passage of Scripture, or a time of prayer. These slivers are not the full glory of God we long to see, but God is still present, even in the cleft of the rock.

Present to Be Known

The Moses Principle also applies to God. God could have just said no to Moses' request to see his glory. But God didn't reject the request; he amended it. In amending Moses' request, God actually added to it. "I will make all my goodness pass before you and will proclaim before you my name 'The LORD'" (Ex. 33:19). God was going to tell Moses his name. More was going to show Moses more.

In Exodus 3, God had already told Moses one version of his name. It was "I AM" (v. 14). In each encounter Moses shared with God between the burning bush and the cleft of the rock, more wanted more. Moses wanted to see more of God. And God wanted to reveal more of himself to Moses. The name of God first spoken at the burning bush was about to be lengthened.

You may be surprised, however, by what God called himself:

The LORD, the LORD, a God merciful and gracious, slow to anger, and abounding in steadfast love and faithfulness, keeping stead-fast love for thousands, forgiving iniquity and transgression and sin, but who will by no means clear the guilty, visiting the iniq-uity of the fathers on the children and the children's children, to the third and the fourth generation. (Ex. 34:6–7)

That is God's name. (And by the way, this is the longest self-description of God in the entire Bible.) In this encounter, God didn't just want Moses to see him, but to know him.

Don't miss this: God wants to be known, not just experienced.

His presence bears purpose. We often just want to feel, witness, see, and touch. But God wants to be known. He wants our minds and our hearts. When we ask God for his presence, our human nature can get caught up in the goose bumps, the exhilaration, and the ecstasy. God knows this about us, and he knew it about Moses. That is why God added to Moses' request. God wanted to give Moses knowledge, not just experience. God wanted to give Moses more than he asked for.

The presence of God is not just about awe and wonder. God doesn't just draw near to reveal himself to us in glory. God's presence is also about knowledge. God wants to be known. When my wife and I hang out, we don't just bask in each other's presence. We don't just stare at each other from across the dinner table. We talk. My wife and I share knowledge about ourselves. Being present with each other means sharing what is going on inside of us. Presence is the sharing of knowledge.

God wants a relationship of shared knowledge with you, not just shared experience. If to you God's presence is just about experience, you are missing out on what God is trying to give you when he draws near. God is not a silent idol, present only to look at and ogle over. God is a speaking force who is present to share his very self. How should this change your perception of God's presence? How does this revise the reasons you might seek out the nearness of God? When you ask for God's presence, are you seeking to know him more or simply gather more experiences? When you feel as if you are in more of God's presence, are you discovering more of God? After all, the good news of God's presence is that we get to know more of God.

A Jealous God

Let's zoom out from Moses' mountaintop experience and see what was happening with the huge crowd of Israelites waiting at the mountain's foot. When Moses first went up onto Mount Sinai to enter God's presence, the rest of Israel was left in absence.[4] While Moses was engulfed in the cloud of God's nearness, what were the people surrounded by absence doing? After all, many of us can't relate to Moses on the mountain. We have a lot more in common with the people who were left behind. They had to stay and wait while they watched Moses go up and experience God.

It's not as if the Israelites couldn't see the huge cloud of fire on the mountain's peak or hear the loud cracks of noise ripping through the air. The Israelites could even hear God's voice from time to time.[5] They could see Moses in God's presence but weren't invited into it. I have often had times when everyone around me seemed to be connecting with God, while all I could do was sit idly by and watch them. What is our response to these moments of absence? What was Israel's response?

The golden calf was Israel's response. The Israelites had just had a series of extremely spiritual encounters. They had seen the plagues, fled Egypt through a split Red Sea, and witnessed God descend upon a mountain as thick smoke. Moses was away from the camp for a long time with God, and no one knew when their next spiritual encounter would be. So the Israelites fashioned for themselves an idol of gold in the form of a calf. They filled up the distance between them and God with idolatry. In their feelings of absence, they wanted more.

We do the same thing today. In our pursuit of more, we often look to substitutes that promise us the feelings of nearness we desire. We forsake the presence of God for the presence of pleasure. Just like Israel at the foot of the mountain, we are far too easily satisfied with idols.

Pastor and theologian Timothy Keller defined idolatry as "taking some incomplete joy of this world and building your entire life on it." Keller said that idolatry "turns the good thing into an absolute that overturns every other allegiance or value."[6] Idolatry is when we take any thing and make it everything. More wants more, but on its own terms. More wants more of the god it has designed.

Left unchecked, the Moses Principle can lead us astray. In our journey for more of God, we end up wanting more than God. So we look to substitutes that promise us the feelings of nearness we desire. When we are experiencing absence, any promise of presence is appealing. Many things promise to fill the absence we feel. These are idols.

We want idols to be present where God is absent. However, they are inevitably unsuccessful because these momentary golden statues cannot fill the gap left by an eternal God. The shoes of the Almighty are too big for idols to fill. Absence is incurable when idols are the remedy. Israel found that out the hard way.

At God's command, Moses disciplined the people for their betrayal. He actually melted down the idol, ground it to dust, sprinkled the gold powder into the people's water, and made them drink it.[7] Like metal that doesn't belong in our guts, idolatry eventually turns our hearts sour and sick.

After the incident with the golden calf, while God was still talking to Moses and passing all his goodness in front of him, God warned Moses about the dangers of idolatry: "Do not worship any other god, for the LORD, whose name is Jealous, is a jealous God" (Ex. 34:14 NIV).

Wait a minute! Just a few verses ago, God told Moses he was going to proclaim the divine name. We have already looked at the long, beautiful, and descriptive name God gave himself. But now God says his name is "Jealous." God's name is Jealous with a capital J. Why? Is he self-conscious, pitiable, needy, clingy, or fearful? No. God's jealousy is about what God most wants: to give us himself.

The love God has for us is so strong that when we give our affections to something other than him, a holy jealousy arises in his person. When we worship anything other than God, we rob ourselves of our greatest satisfaction. God is jealous for our joy and his glory.

God is not jealous in the way you and I are. He is passionate about lifting up the best thing in the universe. He is determined to make the main thing the main thing, and God is the main thing. So when we do not make God the main thing in our lives, he experiences jealousy on our behalf. When God is not the center of our lives, we rob ourselves of our ultimate joy. God wants to fix that. This desire in God is called jealousy. Jealousy is God's good desire to give us the best thing in the world—himself. Jealousy is God's good desire to make great the greatest thing—himself.

Shining Faces

After God had passed all his goodness in front of Moses and had spoken to him the divine name, Moses went back down to the people of Israel who were waiting at the foot of the mountain. As he descended the slope of Mount Sinai, the people were afraid to come near him. Moses didn't know it, but his face was shining because he had been with the Lord. This was undeniable, visible proof that Moses had been in God's presence. He was radiant from the encounter. The imprint of God's presence with Moses was evident to all. The experience didn't just stay on the mountaintop; it followed him into the camp.

Encountering God's presence can leave a mark on us. Not just an inward mark, but a mark that anyone looking at us can see. Second Corinthians 3:1–18 shows how this can happen.

In this passage, the apostle Paul takes us back to Moses on the mountain with God. We see a picture of Moses coming off the mountain, face shining and those famous stone tablets scooped up in his arms. Chiseled on the stone slates, by God's hand, was the Law. Paul called the Law carved on those chunks of rock "the ministry of death" and "the ministry of condemnation."[8]

The Law received this name because it set a standard that humans cannot reach and announced the punishment of death upon those who fall short. Yet the words carved on these stone tablets were glorious, and Moses' encounter with their author radiated throughout his face. After a while, Moses began to put a veil over his face because its shining scared people.

We do not have tablets of stone, but we have something better. Paul explained that now God does not use his mighty hand to write on rock but on the tablets of our hearts. God engraves his new covenant on the flesh of our inner beings. His words are no longer outside of us, condemning us with the ministry of death. His words are inside us, confirming us in his ministry of life.

Our faces do not shine like Moses' did. That was only the outward residue of glory, like an echo reverberating off cave walls. We have something better. The glory that rested on Moses faded away, but the glory we receive is permanent and permeated.

If the ministry that brought condemnation was glorious, how much more glorious is the ministry that brings righteousness! For what was glorious has no glory now in comparison with the surpassing glory. And if what was transitory came with glory, how much greater is the glory of that which lasts! (2 Cor. 3:9–11 NIV)

The glory earned for us in Christ and written on our hearts by the Holy Spirit will not fade away like a dying echo. It is an eternal glory. Furthermore, it does not just affect our faces. The far-surpassing glory of Christ radiates through our whole beings— body, mind, and soul.

The radiating glory of Jesus Christ in us does more than shine through our pores; it transforms who we are. And what is it transforming us into? The glory of Christ is changing us into the image of Christ. The more we look like Jesus, the more our faces shine.

> And we all, with unveiled face, beholding the glory of the Lord, are being transformed into the same image from one degree of glory to another. For this comes from the Lord who is the Spirit. (2 Cor. 3:18)

God is making his glory visible in us. God is becoming more present to the world as we are transformed into the image of God. No wonder Jesus said we are the light of the world.[9] As we behold Jesus, with our faces unveiled, the Holy Spirit remakes us, bit by bit, into the image of Jesus. The more we conform to the image of Christ, the more present God becomes in our own lives and the lives of those around us. Let us come off Mount Calvary, meeting Jesus on his cross, and enter the camps of this world with shining faces so that people can look at us and say, "You have been with God."

Because there is one more party to which the Moses Principle applies: the world wants more of God. They may not know it, but everyone is longing for God. And it is our encounter with Jesus that equips us to give the world what it most desires.

FIVE

THE FAR-OFF PROMISES
OF AN ELUSIVE GOD

Why must Christians wait?

*For the grace of God has appeared, bringing
salvation for all people, training us to renounce
ungodliness . . . in the present age, waiting for
our blessed hope, the appearing of the glory
of our great God and Savior Jesus Christ.*
—TITUS 2:11–13

Nothing good can come from that place." These were the first words I heard concerning my destination after landing at the New Delhi airport in India. It was December 2012, and India was anything but wintery. My hosts informed me that I should pack a sweater, but that ended up just being extra luggage. I was completely alone in the world's second-most populated country and was just told by my taxi driver that the place I was headed was known for crime, gangs, and dead ends.

"Nothing good comes out of that place," he repeated in good English through his thick accent. I was headed out to a rural town in India that was home to millions of people, whose language had not yet received a version of the Bible. I wish I could be more specific about the details of my trip, but due to the violent persecution going on in India toward Bible translators I must keep the specifics obscure.

The Seed Company, an amazing Bible translation charity, had sent me over to visit this people group and write about my experience. The mission of the Seed Company is to translate God's Word into the languages of every people group on earth. At the time of my trip, there were still one billion people without God's Word in their own tongue. Though the fact was staggering, it wasn't real to me until I met an entire civilization that had never heard God speak their language through the Bible.

After taking three different planes to New Delhi, another domestic plane, and a three-hour car ride riddled with uneven dirt roads, I finally made it to this Bibleless people group. I met up with the leader of the effort in the area as well as my translator. They began describing the situation and the area to me.

The local speakers of this language were ashamed to speak their language anywhere outside their own villages. Their native tongue was seen as too simplistic and casual by those who spoke the national language of Hindi. Great shame lies with a people who have never had their own dialect validated. The songs they sing to their children, the way they say "I love you" to their spouses, and even the words they use in their own thoughts are seen as not good enough. These people were marginalized. But by translating the Bible into their mother tongue, humans weren't just validating this people group, God was.

After only being there a few minutes, I learned that nearly three-fourths of this language's speakers were illiterate. This was disheartening to hear, considering the effort was centered on the written word. But my concerns melted away with the Indian sun when the leader of the project showed me something called a Proclaimer Box. It was a black, rectangular box with two speakers and buttons in between them. The Proclaimer Box was about the size of a shoebox if you sat the box up on its longest side.

This solar-powered boom box could be loaded up with audio recordings of any Bible translation and played loudly enough for an entire village to hear. A translation of the beginning of Genesis was stored on the box's hard drive.

Before I could even put down my bags, we took the Proclaimer Box out into a village. Most of the people were already gathered around a traveling snake charmer looking to score some quick cash before heading to the next town. Not even the snake charmer spoke the local language. But as soon as we hit Play on the Proclaimer Box and the people heard their own language pour out of it, the crowd shifted to us. God was unashamedly speaking to the language of the people.

I sat there as the Genesis creation account was relayed to the villagers. I saw people who believed in the hundreds of gods of Hinduism stare in amazement as the Proclaimer Box told them that the one true God created absolutely everything through his Word—the words they were now hearing in their mother tongue.

After the box finished transmitting the opening chapters of Genesis, my translator began to ask through another translator what the people thought of these words. One woman spoke up. The message hurdled over three language barriers to get to me. "I always thought there was one true God," she said, "but I didn't know it was true until I heard him speak to me in my own language." Seldom, if ever, had this people group had an encounter with God. But now, since his Word was in their own language, they could connect with their one true Creator.[1]

The term *people group* has never been the same to me since. These people had their own way of life, their own customs, their own land, and their own language. For the first time in my life, the magnitude of Revelation 7:9 struck me: "I looked, and there before me was a great multitude that no one could count, from every nation, tribe, people and language, standing before the throne and before the Lamb" (NIV).

God is building a family. His presence is for his people. God will move into our neighborhood and all those who are in the people group of God will dwell with him. This has always been God's plan. He is gathering a people for himself one word at a time.

No village is too remote, no people too primitive, no language too outmoded or unused. Every nation, tribe, people, and language will be represented in heaven, and I was seeing some of my first brothers and sisters from this remote Indian village join the family.

The promise of all nations living in the immediate presence of God should feed the hope of every Christian. Those of every color and tongue called out by the Word of God and saved by the blood of Christ will someday stand in the light of God's presence for all eternity. This is the future of God's people. We look forward to the creation of a new family, a new people group that will live in God's land, in God's presence, forever. But we aren't to the end yet.

A Wandering People Group

Like all stories, the tale of God's people group has a beginning, and that beginning started with presence. Genesis 12 picks up the narrative of God's work with a man named Abram—or as we more affectionately called him in the VBS songs of my childhood, "Father Abraham." In some kind of magnificent, unique, and rare way, God became present to Abram.

If you've ever seen *Monty Python and the Holy Grail*, you'll remember the scene where a horribly caricatured version of God parts the clouds to speak to King Arthur. The king and his men are galloping about to the sound of coconuts banging together, which is supposed to mimic the sound of horse hooves, when a clap of thunder and a booming voice come from the sky. The voice is deep, ominous, and full of vibrato, "Arthur, Arthur, King of the Britons!" At this, the company halts their imaginary horses and falls to their knees to grovel. Then in a harsher, more shrill tone, God says, "Oh, don't grovel! If there's one thing I can't stand, it's people groveling!"[2]

The crass British comedy troop is poking fun at the presumed "religious encounter with God." There is always some heavenly preamble or call, followed by a falling to the ground by the one being addressed. This is not what happened to Abram. God didn't open up their dialogue with an "Abram, Abram, Son of Terah!" God just started right in with a shocking command.

No matter how abrupt they might have been, the words God used in his first address to Abram are some of the first and most significant in the story of God's people group: "Go from your country and your kindred and your father's house to the land that I will show you. And I will make of you a great nation" (Gen. 12:1–2).

God was calling Abram out of every sense of identity he had. God called Abram out of his "country," stripping him of any national identity. God called Abram out of his "kindred," taking away any family ties or allegiances he had. Finally, God got specific and called him out of his "father's house," removing even the connection to his very home. Every shred of earthly, geographical, or genealogical associations Abram might have been tempted to hold on to were now made absent to him.

Abram was no longer from Ur, no longer a Chaldean, and no longer part of the house of his father, Terah. He had been set apart for the people group of God, the "great nation" of the Lord.

Abram did not belong to the earth any longer. He had a new home, a new family, and a new country. But he did not have it yet. It was as if Abram and his family packed up everything they owned in a U-Haul and headed off for a new home. Except Abram's entire life would be the drive between the two places.

He would indeed arrive to this promised land, but not in his earthly life. It wasn't as if he just had to drive the moving van across the country for a few days. His life was a sojourn, a journey, and a wandering. He didn't belong in the home he had left, and he didn't belong in the U-Haul. His home was always ahead of him and always absent.

Christians live in the same situation. When Jesus becomes our Lord, he calls us to a new home—his home. We no longer belong to this world. We are on a journey. When God becomes present to us, the world becomes absent. We are a wandering people.[3]

The Presence That Creates Absence

Abram hears this promise and command from God, which is miraculous all by itself. What's even more remarkable is that Abram did exactly what God told him to do. He went! God gave Abram such a potent whiff of his presence that Abram was ready to do whatever God asked. In this way, God's presence is powerful not only in his own divine might but in his personal influence. When God becomes present to a human, everything else becomes absent.

The presence of God made Abram absent to the world. God promised Abram that he would inherit a new land and fill it with countless offspring, and Abram believed.

I can't help but think about the Bible translators I met in India. They were a small team of three brilliant minds from the more affluent cities of India. These translators held PhDs in linguistics and literature. They could have gone on to work in any number of important roles that would have been more comfortable, more stable, and more prosperous. But they became absent to every other opportunity because the call of God became present to them. They received a call, like Abram, to leave their normal lives for the sake of another people group.

They moved to a land that wasn't theirs, to learn a language they didn't know, so that they might see the fulfillment of a promise they could not yet behold. The translators were sojourners and exiles in this city. They were not at home, but they were at work. They could not see the finished translation of this new Bible yet, but they believed that God would be true to his Word—that all languages would hear his voice. The presence of God's promise made them absent to the world.

We, too, are citizens, but we are also strangers. We are God's people, but we are also aliens. His presence leads us out, but his absence leads us to wander. His relational presence tells us we have a homeland, but his actual absence tells us we are currently sojourners to that land. Like Abram, we have received a promise that will be fulfilled, but the presence of that promise has made us absent to the world. Not that we are aloof, unconcerned, detached, or uncaring about the affairs and condition of our world—for we care deeply. But we do know that we are not yet with our full family and are not yet dwelling in our true homeland.

The presence of promise leads to a realization of absence. We have been promised that our family, home, and God are elsewhere, up ahead, and we will feel the sting of their absence until we enter into them.

Unqualified for Presence

You know that kid who always got picked last for dodge ball—the one who made the team captain's eyes roll when their lot fell on him for the last pick? I was that kid—out of shape, not very fast, and a bit of a liability to the team. The team captains were always the most athletic, most popular, and most skilled kids in the school. So they ended up picking those most like themselves first. Those without their prowess for catching, throwing, and running were the crumbs off the table that the gym teacher's stare forced the captains to pick up.

We tend to think that God works the same way. Since God is perfectly good and holy, we expect him to pick people who are good and holy for his team. Surely the people group of God is filled with the best and the brightest. But this just isn't true.

Abram didn't come from a holy family—or even a God-fearing family. It wasn't his righteousness that caught God's eye. Abram came from a pagan nation of idol worshippers. Furthermore, if fathering a nation was to be God's chief concern, Abram should have been the last choice. God made a promise to Abram, saying, "I will make of you a great nation," but Abram's wife, Sarai, was barren![4] How could Abram be the father of a huge family if his wife couldn't get pregnant?

Nothing about who Abram was or what he could do earned God's presence or God's promise, but both came nonetheless. Abram was just as absent from God as anyone else, but God, by his own initiative, became present.

The promise that God made to Abram was for what would eventually become the nation of Israel. Like Abram, they were not chosen as God's people group because they were special or had earned it. In fact, the Bible tells us that the exact opposite is true.

Deuteronomy 7:7 says, "It was not because you were more in number than any other people that the LORD set his love on you and chose you, for you were the fewest of all peoples." We do not earn the presence and the promise of God. Instead, it is God who sets his love upon us.

I guarantee you that the Seed Company did not choose to translate God's Word into a local Indian dialect because that particular people group had earned the privilege. It was because God had willed that every language would have a chance to hear his gospel that the work began in India. The Bible would have been translated into their language whether or not they deserved it, showed any interest in it, or outperformed another people group. These people got the Bible because it was God's will. God became present to this people group, not because of their goodness, but because of his promise. Every tribe and every language will be a part of God's people group.

The people group of God's presence is not limited to those who are in good moral, societal, economical, or familial standing. God comes close to whomever he chooses. You might think that God feels absent to you because you are not worthy of his presence. You may think that you don't come from the right part of town or that you have done something far too terrible for God to forgive. But God draws near to those who are far.

God can be present to us even though we are absent to him. The Indian locals said nothing good can come from that place, and yet God still moved into the neighborhood. I promise that even if you believe nothing good can come out of you, God can still move incredibly close to you. But sometimes, like Abram, we do attempt to establish presence by our own strength.

The purpose God has for your life far supersedes who you are, what you have done, and how you feel. It was God's intention for Abram's life that established the covenant and called for his presence. God's own desire brought himself to Abram. Presence is not something we earn. Abram did nothing to deserve the presence and promise of God.

Manufacturing Presence

It's silly to point out, but having a kid takes a two-person team. I'm not here to give you a biology lesson, but Sarai was as much a part of this whole "fathering a nation" thing as Abram was. Imagine how hard it must have been for Sarai. She didn't go star gazing with God. She wasn't visited by the Word of the Lord in a dream. The covenant was not spoken to her. It was all delivered secondhand by her husband.

She hadn't experienced the presence, but she'd been swept up into fulfilling the promise. Could you picture Abram, coming in off the front lawn after God first appeared to him, shouting, "Sarai! Pack up the house! Gather all our belongings! We're moving."

Sarai would have surely been startled. "Why? Where are we going?"

To which Abram may have replied, "I don't know, but God spoke to me out on the porch!"

How hard it must have been for Sarai to follow Abram away from home and family on some mission of blind trust. All the while, Abram would have been telling her, "You're going to have a baby. God promised." How much doubt would have filled her heart each month when she discovered, yet again, that she was barren?

For any couple that has unsuccessfully tried to have children for years, you already know the severe levels of suffering and doubt Abram and Sarai must have been going through. Most likely, God did not audibly or visibly reveal himself to you and promise you that you would have a nation of children, and yet the pain caused by each negative pregnancy test is unbearable.

How much worse it must have been for Abram and his wife to have seen and heard the living God give them the promise of children, only to go through ten years of waiting, a decade of darkness. The promise was present, but its fulfillment was absent. That is why presence breeds absence. Because it reveals a reality that is not yet present and makes us remain in a time when it is absent.

Where is God? Abram and Sarai must have constantly thought. They knew God could speak; they knew he could make himself seen. Then why wasn't he attending to them in their hour of need? Why wasn't he answering their petition for the fulfillment of his promise? Is God absent? Is God not there?

When things go this wrong, we tend to try to solve them using our own methods. Think of a banker who was promised a $2,000 bonus in the future. The banker is excited about the bonus and waits for it patiently. After a long time, longer than the banker intended to wait, a travesty strikes the banker's family and puts them in financial trouble. The banker asks his boss about the bonus, and the boss ensures him that it is forthcoming. But the banker can wait no longer. So he decides to steal $2,000 from the bank's vault, promising himself that when the bonus check comes, he just won't cash it. Instead of waiting on the promise, he fulfills it himself.

Abram and Sarai made such a mistake when they decided to take the matter of God's absence into their own hands. Sarai reasoned that if God had promised Abram children and she was barren, then God must have wanted the children to come through another woman.[5] So Sarai instructed Abram to attempt making a child with one of their servants, Hagar. If God was going to be absent, Sarai would make his promise present. They were going to cash a check God had not yet written.

So Abram slept with Hagar, and they conceived a child, who was given the name Ishmael. Though God had been breathtakingly present with Abram in the past, his absence in the present was too overwhelming. God was not working in the way, or within the time frame, Abram and Sarai wanted, so they tried to create what they weren't experiencing. Something had to be done. But Abram's attempt to manufacture the presence and promise of God was unsuccessful. Hagar would not be the one who would bring about God's chosen people group.

This is the mistake we make in our faith. We know the promises God has made to us and we want them now. God says that he will wipe away every tear, so we try to create complete comfort and ease in this life. God promises that we will have treasure in heaven, so we store up for ourselves treasure on earth. God declares that we will dwell with him and see him as he is, so we claim that we already do.

We manufacture fulfillment to these promises of presence. Misunderstood absence leads to misunderstood presence. Manufactured presence births illegitimate children of absence.

Many of us manufacture presence because we are sick of absence. The college student who hasn't felt God in years fakes her way through a church service instead of grappling with the sting of absence. The successful Christian businessman who can't find God's purpose in his work keeps laboring over longer hours so he can buy more things in a mad attempt to fabricate purpose. The divorced mother of three who is broken inside forces smiles to her face and lies through her lips so she doesn't have to confront her pain in front of others.

Whether faith, purpose, happiness, or something else, we all try to manufacture the presence of something that is actually absent. We do not wait on the promises of God. We try to speak them into existence now. Absence is uncomfortable, so we settle for a false presence. Instead of realizing that God is absent in the way we most desire but present in the way we most require, we manufacture cheap knockoffs of his promises in order to convince us that things aren't as hard as they seem.

God's actual presence must remain as our future hope without being manipulated into a current lie. We must trust the miraculous power of God's relational presence in our lives through Christ while we sojourn here on our way to his home.

Imagine, for instance, if the translators of that small people group's language, after years of hard labor, decided that the work was too hard to finish. So the team of translators decided to simply make up the rest of the translation. Instead of painstakingly translating each word within its context, both scripturally and culturally, they just sped through and added whatever they wanted. The finished Bible would be present, but God's Word would be absent. A manufactured presence is actually absence.

How much of the presence we claim, feel, or hold on to is really manufactured? How much of our man-made presence is created in the lab of religion in order to tone down our anxieties of absence? How much false presence is the result of true impatience? We must wait on God instead of manufacturing him in our image.

Elusive Presence

God continued to be absent even after Ishmael's birth. Abram and Sarai were given new names, Abraham and Sarah, and God renewed his promise and his presence.[6] But Sarah was still not pregnant. They had to wait another fourteen years before giving birth to their son Isaac. That must have been an excruciating waiting period. It was about twenty-five years from the time God promised Isaac to the time Isaac was actually born.[7]

Let me put it this way: if God had given Abraham a kid the same year he gave the promise, that son would have now been out of college and married with his own kids.

This was the normal cycle of presence and absence through which God related to Abraham. God would speak, and then years would pass. God would promise, and nothing would happen. Abraham would move, but God seemed to stay still. Abraham would experience extremely short moments of epiphany and wonder followed by excruciatingly long stretches of silence and doubt. Absence was punctuated by presence, not the other way around. It was absence that made up Abraham's normal day to day as a sojourner toward God.

Abraham did not constantly stand in the glory of God's presence only to slip out of it for a moment of weakness with Hagar. Years of absence ground the gears of Abraham's faith to a halt. Even though he had witnessed one of the most profound revelations of God's presence in all history, Abraham was still worn down by the seemingly endless barrage of absence.

How God related to Abraham is a micro version of the macro way he relates to the world. After Adam and Eve were exiled from the garden, nearly five hundred years passed before God revealed himself to Noah before the great flood. Another four hundred years crept along until God finally spoke to Abraham. The people of Israel had to wait for four hundred years in slavery to Egypt before God spoke through Moses. Israel waited in exile during their Assyrian captivity. The Israelites had to endure Babylonian captivity and exile as well before they could return to their temple and the presence of God.

Individuals, along with the entire world, experience long stretches of absence dotted with short moments of presence. The cycle of God's elusive presence affects us all.

A good way to think about God's elusive presence is to think of it like putting oil in a car. I can drive my car all over town, but every three thousand miles or so I need to give it an oil change. I am always present with my car, driving it, putting gas in it, and airing up the tires. But every so often it needs a different kind of care from me—fresh oil.

God is always present with us, guiding us, teaching us, and correcting us. But every now and then, in order to keep us moving in the direction he wants us to go, he becomes present to us in a different way. God is always behind the wheel, but every so often we can find him under the hood.

Understanding the elusive presence of God in this way does not make God's presence behind the wheel nonexistent, nor does it make his moments under the hood any less overwhelming and magnificent. However, understanding God's presence as the elusive oil change explains a reality we often want to be false. It seems that as soon as we have an encounter with the presence of God, it has slipped through our fingers. As soon as we have peeked at something new of God's glory through the cleft of the rock, the moment has passed us by and we can't quite put our finger on what it was we saw. As soon as we close our eyes in the worshipful cave of Red 2, we open our eyes to the encroaching black trash bags.

Often, God's presence is quick and fleeting, like something glimpsed out the window of a fast-moving train. We know it was real, we saw what it was, but before we have time to hold on to it or capture it, it has sunk behind the caboose.

God's elusive presence is not bad news. It can actually come as a great relief to those who are frustrated by the permanency of absence and the fickleness of presence. Instead of viewing those brief moments of presence as something once had and lost, we can start to view them as sweet respites from the long absence in which we currently dwell.

Moments of presence are not defeated by absence. Instead, absence is conquered by short spurts of presence. Each encounter becomes a new height to which we climb instead of a height from which we fall. You do not have to look back at a great moment of presence in your life and think, *Why isn't God with me now like he was then?* Instead, you can say, "Absence will not overtake me *now*, because God overtook me in presence *then*."

Since we know this is how God works, we should not be surprised to find ourselves in the longest, most important, and very last cycle of absence during this "church age." We live in the period of waiting between the time when Jesus ascended into heaven and when he will return in his second coming. With this knowledge of God's elusive presence, periods of absence become part of God's blueprint for saving the world. We can sojourn through this world as the people group of God because we know this is the time God has allotted for sojourning. While we wait for Jesus' return, we are differing people groups on the way to our ultimate people group.

We stand on the mountaintop of Jesus' first coming and look across the landscape of the future for his second coming. The presence in the first gives us hope in the second. Because he drew near, we do not despair that he now feels far. Waiting is expected. Absence is normal. For what Jesus came and started, he will return to finish.

Begun but Not Complete

Abraham did finally have a son named Isaac. There was great joy for the new parents that day. But in the grand scheme of God's promise, it sure looked like a small accomplishment. Abraham had a son, but not a nation. Sarah did give birth, but not to a people group. The fulfillment of the promise began in the miraculous birth of Isaac, but its completion was still far off. The presence of promise had begun but had not yet been completed.

We experience the promises of God in a very similar way—as begun but not completed; as already but not yet. God promised us that we would dwell with him. Though he did earn us the right to live with him through Jesus' sacrifice, we are not yet in God's house. God promised that there will be no more tears, pain, or death. Though Jesus did take the death we deserved, we still live in pain with the shadow of mortal death looming over us. The promises of God are more certain than the sunrise, but their coming always seems to be over the next horizon.

Here's how the book of Hebrews depicts Abraham and Sarah's faith in the promise of God: "These all died in faith, not having received the things promised, but having seen them and greeted them from afar" (11:13). Abraham and Sarah did not get to see the consummation of what God promised, but they did look forward in faith to what God promised. Their faith wasn't just in God's guarantee of a people group but of a Savior who would come out of that people group.

Abraham had faith in Jesus, even though he didn't know that would be his name. Abraham caught glimpses of the salvation that would come out of the people group he and Sarah began. One of the clearest glimpses was in God testing Abraham by commanding him to sacrifice his treasured son Isaac.

At the command of God, Abraham took his promised son Isaac up a hill to offer him as a sacrifice. This is the child whom God said would lead to the salvation of all nations. But Abraham did not let that deter him. He bound his beloved son and placed him on an altar of wood. Abraham raised a knife to slaughter his son, but God stopped him before he went through with it, saying, "Do not lay your hand on the boy or do anything to him, for now I know that you fear God, seeing you have not withheld your son, your only son, from me" (Gen. 22:12). Then God himself provided a substitute sacrifice, a ram caught in a nearby thicket.

God provides the sacrifice he requires. Abraham had faith that God would do this. Before going up the hill, Abraham said to Isaac, "God will provide for himself the lamb for a burnt offering, my son" (v. 8). And he did. God provided a substitute sacrifice for Abraham and did not make him give up his son. God has provided a substitute sacrifice for us as well, and it is his only Son.

What God did not require of Abraham, the slaughtering of his own son, he required of himself. Jesus, the firstborn Son of God who is God himself in the flesh, gave up his life for us on the cross.

Abraham looked forward to this sacrifice in faith. We look back upon that sacrifice in faith. Abraham did not know what it would look like. We know exactly what it looks like—a cross. But like Abraham, we, too, look forward in faith. We look forward to the day when Jesus will return and take us home.

Just as my taxi driver in New Delhi, India, told me nothing good comes out of that place, someone spoke a similar word about Jesus. "Can anything good come out of Nazareth?" they asked.[8] The city of Nazareth, that people group, was too small and insignificant to be of any real importance. But just as Abraham came out of his people group unto the glory of God, so Jesus came out of his.

But Jesus' original home was not Nazareth, Egypt, or Bethlehem. Jesus' home was at God's side in glory. And like Abraham, Jesus left his home, his family, and his name to start a new people group. This sojourner from that small people group in Nazareth bought, by his blood, the eternal family status of the largest and greatest people group the world will ever see—the people of God.

The New Testament says, "If you are Christ's, then you are Abraham's offspring, heirs according to promise" (Gal. 3:29). What's true for Abraham is true for all followers of Jesus. The promise is ours to inherit, though it is not yet ours to hold. The fulfilled promise we most desire is still far off, but God is still present with us in the way we most require—faithfully bringing about fulfillment for all who claim Christ.

I continue to get updates from my friends in India. The church is growing as more claim Christ. The translators are continuing to toil, and their work is beginning to bear fruit. I now keep in my office a small paperback copy of the gospel of Luke in the language of that Indian people group. The full promise of God's Word has yet to be attained in that Indian village, but God is working through many of his sons and daughters to see its fulfillment.

And someday, alongside all the heirs of Abraham, from every tribe, tongue, and nation, we will experience the fulfillment of God's promise. The presence that has been elusive will show itself as both infinite and definite. All the people groups will cease their traveling and arrive home as the one people group of God.

SIX

SICK WITH LOVE

How do I search for a God who is absent?

> *Behold, the cry of the daughter of my people*
> *from the length and breadth of the land:*
> *"Is the LORD not in Zion?*
> *Is her King not in her?"*
> —JEREMIAH 8:19

My wife and I began dating in high school. This was not your typical boy-meets-girl story. It was more like your classic boy-tricks-girl-into-going-out-with-him-even-though-he's-a-complete-nerd story. My wife, Meagan, was a cheerleader. I collected Pokémon cards. Meagan was popular and pretty. I was the class clown. But I was taken with her.

Ever since we shared a class together our freshman year, she had walked across my heart and left an imprint I had to fill. So one day, in the tenth grade, I worked up the courage to tell Meagan that

I was about to get my first car and that we should go on a date in it. Taking me for the funny guy that I was, she laughed and sarcastically said, "Yeah, sure!" But my romantically naive ears heard the most genuine, "I'd love to."

The next week I went up to her after our American history class and said, "I got my truck yesterday. I'll pick you up at six." What I didn't know was that she was completely caught off guard. I had trapped her into a date she never agreed to. We ended up, despite her reservations and my naivety, having a great time going to dinner and watching a movie. After all, it was opening weekend for the movie *Mean Girls*. We drove around the lake and chatted, and then I dropped her back off at her house. Before saying good night, we agreed to have breakfast together one morning before school at a local café. I was beaming. The prom king and the quarterback had nothing on me! I had a second date with the girl of my dreams.

The morning we met for breakfast at the café finally came. She was wearing a cute white skirt and a pink top with flowers on it. I can still see it. We ordered our food, but before it came she excused herself to go to the restroom. I waited. Five minutes went by. Ten minutes went by. Our food came. Was she avoiding me? Fifteen minutes went by. *It's over!* I thought. *I've blown it.* Finally, she returned to the table looking flushed. I asked her if everything was all right. Her pale white face began to turn red. Stomach bugs are hard to explain on a date. "Sorry I was in there so long," she said. "I was throwing up."

Despite Meagan's digestive disaster, which I can tell you really sets the mood for a breakfast date, I still continued to pursue her. After all, a little indigestion wasn't going to keep me from my dream girl. Throughout the rest of our time in high school and even into college, I sought this girl. I discovered more about her. I was interested in her interests. Where she went, I went. If she felt far from me, I did all that I could to close that relational gap. If things weren't going smoothly, I would try to smooth them out. There was a wife in her and a husband in me, and I was dedicated to searching them both out.

Two people falling in love is one of the best tales that can be told. One of my favorite stories of the pursuit of love is found in the Bible, in the book Song of Solomon. Though I know it was a stomach bug that made our second date an awkwardly memorable one, I prefer to think that Meagan wasn't sick with an illness, but, like the woman in Song of Solomon, was sick with love.

Sick with Love

What it looks like to be sick with love is modeled for us in Song of Solomon. This strikingly erotic biblical book chronicles the romantic love relationship between King Solomon and a woman, who serves as the primary speaker of the book.[1] Like any good love story, the book has its ups and downs. There are beautiful moments of presence and painful moments of absence.

For thousands of years this book has been understood in a variety of ways, but one of its chief understandings has been as an allegory of the relationship between humans and God. God can be present and absent to us in a variety of different ways, and there may be no better place in our Bible to delve more deeply into this than the Song of Solomon.

In this book we do not have straightforward theology but a love story. We do not have catechisms but caresses. We do not have dogma but devotion. What better place could there be to help us understand the rapturous elation caused by presence and the deep pain inflicted by absence than in the subtleties of a love story?

The story begins with a proclamation of love. The woman confesses her love for Solomon, and Solomon confesses his love for her.[2] The king throws a party for his beloved in his banquet hall.[3] The festivities and adoration she receives from the king cause a confusing emotion to arise within her. She begins to feel overcome by love to the point of exhaustion, weakness, and illness.

"Sustain me with raisins," she says, "refresh me with apples, for I am sick with love" (Song 2:5). The woman Solomon loves is so consumed by affection that she is ill with it. Her fondness is making her faint. The king's nearness is making her knees weak. A blissful disease has taken her body, and the only cure is deeper intimacy with the king. It may not have been this type of rapturous love that drove my wife to run to the café restroom that morning, but I like to think it was.

Presence creates a pain that only more presence can heal. An encounter with God's general or relational presence leaves deep imprints on our souls, like a footprint on a trail, and we spend our lives trying to find the foot it goes with. The tracks of God leave their mark on us. That indentation on the soft ground of our hearts leaves an empty space in its wake. Presence leaves a deeper impression than it fills. The trace of what we have encountered makes us ache to find that which has passed us by.

If you have ever been in love, you already know what this feels like. To be in the presence of the one you love, while still wanting to be more present than the situation allows. You can be hanging out with someone you have a crush on, but still want to have a closer dating relationship with this person. You can be on a date with your boyfriend or girlfriend, but still want to share a deeper commitment. You can be engaged, but still long for your wedding day. You can be married, but still desire to draw closer and closer to your husband or wife. You can be in God's presence here on this earth, but still find yourself sick with the desire to stand before him face-to-face. God's presence can make us sick with love.

You may feel as if you have been searching after God for a long time. Perhaps you have just begun to think about what it means to seek God out. Whether you are far down your journey's path or standing at its threshold wondering if you should begin, I want you to know that the tracks of God put each of us on a lifelong search.

If you are feeling faint and tired in your pursuit of God, remember that you may just be sick with love. The closer you get to your goal, the more desirous it will become. Like Solomon's lover sitting in his banquet hall, you are so near to God that you are sick with it.

On the other hand, if you feel as if the search for God is more than you can bear, I want you to realize that it is far better to be sick in love than healthy in hate. Searching after God is the most fulfilling endeavor you could ever begin. Keep looking for God, search through the sickness, and know that it is God's ever-increasing nearness that puts us in such a fever.

"I Sought Him, but Found Him Not"

I can't stand it when I'm frantically looking for something that ends up being right next to me. Like when I'm running around the house looking for my keys, turning over every couch cushion, just to realize that the keys were hooked to my belt loop the whole time. Or when I'm standing in an aisle of the grocery store and I ask the clerk where I might find the condiments, only to look behind me and see a wall of Heinz staring back. That is almost the impression we get at the first major moment of absence recorded in the Song of Solomon.

After the sublime banquet and her lovesickness, the woman awakens in her bed, thinking that Solomon will be lying next to her. But the king is not where she left him. Her beloved is not where he had been before. The one her heart loves is not where she expects him to be. So before even getting out of bed to see if Solomon might be using the restroom, the woman exclaims, "I sought him, but found him not" (Song 3:1).

It is almost comical how quickly the beloved woman of Solomon exclaims that the king cannot be found. She has only just waked, she is still in bed, and she has already come to two conclusions: (1) she has been on a search and (2) the king cannot be found. She looked in the first and only place she thought Solomon would be, right next to her, and upon discovering his absence, she concludes that her search has been sufficient and her results are conclusive.

Maybe you feel like God is absent. You've looked for him in the places where you thought he would be, but you've come up empty. You may have given up your search for God too soon. I can promise you this: you have not looked for God in every place in which he may be found.

There are beds of scriptures you have not yet pulled back the sheets on. There are doors of prayers you haven't yet opened. You need not exclaim God's absence after a Sunday slump. You don't have to throw up your hands in frustration after a quick season of unanswered prayer.

We must neither be too hasty in our declaration that God is absent, nor too quick to abandon the search for our absent God. If you are going through a dry spell in your relationship with God, do not be so quick to abandon your search for him. If you feel like your search has gone on far too long, do not be so quick to judge that you have looked for him in every place but your own bed.

Jiggling the Latch

After the night of absence, the bride awakens to her wedding day. The two lovers move from being "sick with love" to being "drunk with love." However, as soon as the wedding ends and the marriage has been consummated, the bride awakens again to another episode of absence.[4] She has been bathed in the trappings of a king's honeymoon. Covered in myrrh, cleaned from head to toe, the woman is nestled in her marriage bed. But a knock comes at the door.

It is the king, her husband, and he is asking that his new bride open the locked door for him. She explains that she would get up, but she has removed her garment and does not wish to put it back on. She has bathed her feet and does not wish to get them dirty again.

But the king jiggles the latch. The anticipation of his entry makes the new bride leap from her bed. The jiggling latch promises nearness. She is eager for presence. At the sound of the latch knocking about in its locked hold, the woman declares, "My heart was thrilled within me" (Song 5:4). However, as soon as she opens the door to welcome her husband, the entryway is empty. Her king is absent.

The woman describes her pain: "My soul failed me when he spoke. I sought him, but found him not; I called him, but he gave no answer" (v. 6). Something as near as God's voice can still make our hearts fail if he is not found outside the doors we open for him. The husband with whom she had recently laid was now gone. The man who had just knocked at the door was now completely out of earshot.

As we saw with Abraham, God's presence is elusive. In one moment we are nearer to him than ever, and the next he is no longer in our chambers. One moment he is jiggling the handle of our souls, asking to come in, and the next we swing the door open to find it empty. As Harvard professor of comparative religions Francis Clooney worded it, "He allows himself to be held, but not detained. . . . He can be tantalizingly near, yet is ever just beyond her grasp."[5]

It is God's presence that makes us so sick with love that we spring from our beds. And it is God's absence that makes us so sick with love that we crave him more than ever before.

Lovesickness can be felt in many circumstances. When God is no longer felt in the places we once easily found him, we can be sick with love. When the nearness of God used to feel like sharing a bed, but now feels like he is just jiggling the handle to our door, we can be sick with love. When we simply notice that we long to see God face-to-face, but only experience him in the small peeks our human bodies can tolerate, we can be sick with love.

However, we must not let lovesickness lead us to desperation but to pursuit. The tracks left by presence must not lead us to exhaustion but exhilaration. Your feelings of absence do not speak a word of hate but a word of love. Feeling far from God is not always the punishment of a relationship severed; it could be the evidence of a relationship formed.

Song of Solomon shows us that God's absence is more pursuit than abandonment. It is more the leading of a lover than the leaving of a father. We are sick, not with absence, but with love. And that love sends us on a search.

Absence Makes the Heart Grow Fonder

When something goes missing, we look for it. When your dog runs away, you take to the streets. You look down every alley and road. You put up signs and offer rewards. You leave no stone unturned. That is what the woman in Song of Solomon does when she realizes that her beloved is not in the place she expected him to be.

The footprints of the one she loves are leading out the door, so she follows them into the city. She is looking everywhere throughout the town, asking every passerby and even security guards if they have seen any hint of her love (5:7–8). She doesn't let her premature conclusion of absence or her unfulfilled expectation of presence deter her from tracking down that which she esteems as most precious. She was near the king once. She would be near him again.

Presence lost creates a longing greater than presence had. A singer who loses his voice will treasure it much more when it returns. An athlete who tears her ACL will be all the more thankful when she regains full mobility. A pet once lost won't be taken for granted once it's found.

Why was the king wandering in the streets when he was expected to be present with the woman in bed? Why, after such a profound experience at the banquet and being sick with love, would the king withdraw from the woman and make her experience such an intense feeling of absence? Why does God seem to be so far off just after we have drawn nearer to him than ever before? When we have God right where we want him, why does he take off in the middle of the night? Because absence breeds desire.

God does not withdraw from us for the sake of malice, but for the sake of movement. Absence is a mighty staff in the hand of our Good Shepherd, and God uses it to wisely guide us.

Footprints in the dirt lead us on a chase of desire. The old saying is very true: absence does make the heart grow fonder. In the moments of God's absence, he places space between us, so that in our desperation we may desire him all the more. God utilizes absence to make us more desirous of his presence. The absence of God is not suspension, but seduction. The absence of God allures us into the presence of God. Not only that, but the absence of God may actually be more of an opportunity for faith than you may have first realized.

What Does It Mean to Search for God?

During my long trip through India, I ran into a number of different people who were in that country to "find themselves." Some told me they were going to Calcutta to find God. Others explained that they had to get out of their comfort zones in order to search for God out in the world. Searching for God is a narrative that resonates loudly in our culture. We want an exotic "Eat, Pray, Love" experience. Something has been impressed upon our hearts, and we want to track it down.

This is exactly what the woman in the Song of Solomon did each time she found her king to be missing. When she woke up after the banquet and "found him not," Solomon's beloved leapt from her bed and took to the streets. After Solomon jiggled the handle of her bedchamber door but was not found when the door was opened, she ran out into the streets again. When her beloved went missing, she went out on a search. Absence leads to searching. But it is a unique type of search that God's absence sends us on.

Think of the woman's logic that sent her on this search. It's partially flawed. She didn't need to leave her house, go out into the streets, and search every nook and cranny. Surely the king would have returned to her in time, probably that very night. He never would abandon her or his kingdom.

The woman didn't really need to go out and search, but she had to. Absence made her search. The lack of her lover's presence gnawed at her inner being, begging her to spring to her feet and scour the city for what had been lost. Absence tugged at her like a rope around her gut.

Absence makes us search as well. But the idea of searching for God can be a bit mystical sounding at best and completely impractical at worst. When we stumble upon a season of absence, we begin to search for what we once had. We try attending different churches, reading different books, visiting exotic places, or adopting new habits. We believe that if we look hard enough, we will find God again. The absence of God puts us on a search for God. But how are we to understand and partake in this search for our missing otherworldly other?

We must start by understanding that calling our pursuit of God a "search" can be misleading in a few ways. There are two key components of a search that do not fit with a healthy understanding of our search for God. These two components are duration and direction.

First, since our pursuit is never ending, calling it a search is a misnomer. Calling something a search usually assumes one of two outcomes with regard to the search's duration. Either the object being searched for will be found, effectively ending the search, or the energies, patience, or resources of the searcher will be exhausted, bringing the search to its end. However, our search for God does not end.

God is not a treasure to be found by looking for an X on a treasure map; he can't be dug up once all the paces have been walked. He is not a set of misplaced keys that may be unearthed after retracing our steps and emptying all our drawers. God is too vast to be found in one place. He is not waiting to be discovered under some faraway rock. Even when someone finds God, it is not as if anyone could know him exhaustively.[6]

Even in heaven there will always be more of God to discover. God is infinite, so the search is never ending. Clooney put it this way: "Because we cannot plumb the depths of God, the deeper we fall into God, the less likely we are ever done with searching."[7] Make no mistake, God can be found truly, though we will never be finished finding him fully. Both these promises are good news because they reveal to us that we have embarked on something far greater than a search—we have entered into a never-ending love story.

The second component of our pursuit that makes the word *search* misleading is its direction. Calling the act of pursuing God a search makes it sound as if we are doing the work while God sits idly by waiting to be discovered. This could not be farther from the truth. While our search is necessary, it is not how God is found. People could search all their lives, but if God does not reveal himself to them, he will never be found.[8]

It is God who shows himself to us. It is God who pursues us. It is God who places the desire for his presence in our hearts like bread crumbs down a trail. We may be searching for God, but it is really God drawing us to himself. The direction of our search is from God to us, not from us to God.

The true direction of our search is seen most clearly in Jesus. God did not wait for us in heaven; he came down to us on earth. He did not stay veiled in the clouds; he made himself known as a human being. Our search does not call us to hopelessly grope around the earth until we stumble upon heaven. Our search is the necessary response to the God who is drawing us to himself. So calling our discovery of God a search is a categorical mistake, because it is not we who find God, but God who made himself found in us.

But the word *search* isn't entirely misleading. Searching for God is a necessary part of the Christian life, even though we know its true duration and direction. The search is necessary because when something we love is lost, we must search for it. No one would believe that you loved your pet if you didn't search for it when it ran away. Our searching is necessary because it is the most authentic response to losing something we love.

You can think about our search for God being necessary in the same way a husband's search for his wife is necessary. I still chase after my wife. We both long for deeper intimacy. If I did not search after my wife's heart, it would reveal that I did not truly love her. The search for my wife is the act of marriage.

In the same way, our search for God is the eternal condition of our relationship. It is the organic fruit of one who has had an encounter with God. It is the only genuine response to the genuine presence of God. Searching is necessary because the heart always longs to discover more of God. If God feels absent, our hearts demand that we chase him down.

Do not be discouraged in your search for God. If it begins to feel like you're not going anywhere, remember that the duration of your search is eternal and the direction of your search is heavenly.[9] In doing so you will realize that obtaining all of God is not possible, which makes each piece of him you uncover a joyful step in your never-ending journey toward satisfaction.

However, if you begin to find the search for God needless or burdensome, rediscover the necessity of searching for God by realizing that he is absent. In doing so, you will reawaken a passion to search out that which was once near. God is always present, but ever absent. The more we find of him, the more we discover that we have not yet found.

Faith that attains presence inflames more notices of absence. Clooney's way with words is again helpful: "The hidden one is always here, within. Yet even if this search is unnecessary, it expresses a desire that will never really be quenched."[10] But perhaps no words are more helpful and haunting than the admonition of Psalm 105:4: "Seek the LORD and his strength; seek his presence continually!"

We search for the one who can always be found in order to find the one who will always be hidden. Searching is the Christian life. When we find God, our appetite for his presence is not satisfied, but whetted. As Clooney said elsewhere, our search for God is both "inevitable and impossible."[11] But our search also comes with a promise: "Seek the LORD your God and you will find him, if you search after him with all your heart and with all your soul."[12] Like Solomon's lover, may we leap from our beds of expected presence and take to the streets in our necessary but never-ending search.

Faith in Absence

During the woman's search for her beloved, she came upon some eligible bachelorettes whom she called on for aid. Instead of helping in her search, the bachelorettes question the wandering woman: "What is your beloved more than another beloved, O most beautiful among women? What is your beloved more than another beloved, that you thus adjure us?" (Song 5:9). What is so great about this man of hers? Is he worth all this searching?

She defends her beloved, even in his absence. The beloved woman of Solomon chronicles all the good reasons why her love is better than others. She speaks of all his presence is to her. Describing her beloved's arms, mouth, legs, eyes, and head, she puts all the questions of these skeptical singles to rest. She recounts her beloved's presence in the midst of his absence.

These other women have never seen Solomon and do not know why this woman desires him so much. So the king's beloved takes this opportunity of absence to give testimony to the radiance of the king's presence.

The experience of absence builds one of the most genuine platforms from which to share our testimony of presence. Those who feel far from God, or perhaps have never encountered him at all, are more ready to listen to someone who knows what it feels like when God isn't there. This flips the outward working of absence on its head. Normally, when we feel far from God, we become the cause of concern for all those around us. We are the low ones, seeking counsel and in need of help. But what if the remedy for our absence is also one of the purposes of it? What if we could strengthen our faith in absence while sharing the goodness of God?

Instead of telling everyone how far away God feels, we begin to tell them how close he has come. Instead of telling of his leaving, we tell of his coming. When God feels far, may our mouths open with songs of his nearness. In this way we battle the souring of our own hearts while planting seeds of faith in the hearts of others.

Assurance in Absence

In the Song of Solomon's final story of absence, far less pronounced than the other two, the woman makes one final request of her beloved to help her get through these times of distance: "Set me as a seal upon your heart, as a seal upon your arm" (Song 8:6). She wants a pledge of presence to aid her in times of absence.

I am reminded of the summer before my senior year of college. I had been dating my now-wife for five years and knew that I wanted to propose. But I was going to be working with a church in California for the summer and would not see her for three months. So I decided to propose before our time apart began. I would set a ring on her finger as my seal of presence to help us get through our season of absence. My promise of future nearness would serve as a source of strength for us in our current state of distance.

God has done the same thing for us. He has set his seal on us to help us get through our times of absence. "It is God . . . who has also put his seal on us and given us his Spirit in our hearts as a guarantee" (2 Cor. 1:21–22). God has guaranteed our future by giving us his Spirit in the present. No matter how absent God may feel, we can rest assured that he will make good on his presence's guarantee. We have an assurance in absence, the Spirit of God. God has given us what Solomon's beloved requested.

Love Is Strong As Death

Song of Solomon's love story wraps up with the woman's description of love's ferocity within her.

> Love is strong as death,
> jealousy is fierce as the grave.
> Its flashes are flashes of fire,
> the very flame of the LORD.
> Many waters cannot quench love,
> neither can floods drown it.
> If a man offered for love
> all the wealth of his house,
> he would be utterly despised.
> (8:6–7)

This determined loved one is saying, with no apologies or qualifications, that her love for the king and the king's love for her is stronger than any absence she may face. She likens her love's steadfast grip to the unrelenting hold of death. Just as the grave bears the ultimate violence over human beings, so does her jealousy reign with fierce terror over any competitor.

Absence cannot still her love for Solomon, for her love is a flame that whole oceans of water could not extinguish. For hers is not an affection bought with a dowry or paid for with riches. The love between the king and his beloved is pure for love's sake. It cannot be bought, sold, extinguished, lessened, snuffed out, or done away with. Her love is strong.

As Christians, we, too, have a strong love, a love even stronger than death. Our love is not only an emotional commitment between two parties but an eternal pledge between an infallible God and his chosen bride. This pledge is sealed by the death, burial, and resurrection of Jesus Christ. Our Beloved proved that his love is stronger than death in his resurrection. Jesus showed that his jealousy for our hearts is mightier than the grave's hunger for our flesh. The blood that was lashed out of him in scourging and plunged out of him in crucifixion was his love's flashes of fire that came from his very heart-flame.

No ocean of sin, no flood of time, no onslaught of indifference could quench this love and all it accomplished. Because our love was not bought with even the richest of dowries. Our hand in marriage was paid for by the life of God in the flesh.

How much surer may our love be than the two lovers of the song? How much stronger than death is the love between you and the one who conquered death?

Paul gave Christians their own version of the woman's pledge in Romans 8:35–39:

> Who shall separate us from the love of Christ? Shall tribulation, or distress, or persecution, or famine, or nakedness, or danger, or sword? . . . No, in all these things we are more than conquerors through him who loved us. For I am sure that neither death nor life, nor angels nor rulers, nor things present nor things to come, nor powers, nor height nor depth, nor anything else in all creation, will be able to separate us from the love of God in Christ Jesus our Lord.

The love within us is too strong to be killed, quenched, or bought, for the author of our love has already been killed and has risen again. The perfecter of our love is long-suffering and never changing, so no span of time or space can snuff out his commitment. And the earner of our love has already paid all the costs to bring us to himself, so no one and no thing can offer us a higher price than the one already paid on the cross. When absence becomes overwhelming, remember that we have a love that is stronger than death—the gospel of Jesus Christ.

One final plea from the beloved woman ends the Song of Solomon. The final words of the book read, "Make haste, my beloved, and be like a gazelle or a young stag on the mountains of spices" (8:14). The woman and her king are still absent from each other, so she begs him to make haste in his return. The strength of her love in the king's absence does not blot out the strength of her desire for the king's return. Confidence in absence does not override desire for presence.

We must feel neither condemned nor comfortable in absence. Neither dismay nor distraction should overtake us when God feels far. If we become comfortable in this world, we have stopped our search. If we become defeated in absence, we have forgotten the assurances of God.

We must not be too ready to abandon ourselves to absence nor relinquish our faith in presence. We can stand with the beloved woman of Solomon and say, "Our love is stronger than death," as well as, "Come quickly, Lord!" God withdraws to lead us deeper into himself because he loves us, and by that same love he will return.

THE CHURCH AND GOD'S PRESENCE

When God Isn't There

God has gone.
He has withdrawn.
He's gathered up the train of his holiness,
Stepped back into the plain of his wilderness,
Gone from his estranged wife, his adulteress,
Left though it pains him with brokenness.
God has withdrawn his name from our very midst
And we
Have not even noticed.

We are so focused
On our songs and motions,
On our prayers and tokens,
On our plates and potions,
Now that God has removed his

Glorious closeness
His absence has simply gone unnoticed.
We don't even need God to continue our godly devotions.

Yet these realities have gone unspoken.
For idols have prophesied to our prophets,
Titles have evangelized our evangelist,
And our shepherds and apostles
Are so busy inventing a gospel
That we haven't had the sense
To question,
"Is God even in this?"

We have traded in
The church for an experience,
Put costly grace on clearance,
Forsaken
Hard truth for the mysterious,
Exchanged
A free gift for the meritorious,
Replaced
The foolishness of the cross
With the good news of our own brilliance.

We have exchanged our glorious God
For the worthless idol of our own flesh and blood.

So why are we offended
When we hear that God has relented—
Suspended his presence,

Withdrawn his luminescence from our body of attendance?

Not that he's left us in the lurch
Or that we should forsake the assembly of his body's work,
But maybe we've just given up the search—
Left the death of Golgotha's hill for Olive's resurrection perch.

Which makes one fact unmistakably overt:
It's not God who's withdrawn from us,
It's us who have left him in the dirt.

So let us
Withdraw from our
Sedentary faith to find his preparatory way.
Let us
Withdraw from our
Lies that soothe to find his offensive truth.
Let us
Withdraw from our
Refusal to die to find his endless life.

Let us stop following our way with our truth for our life.

Let us
Withdraw from our way
To find that his will keep us enthralled.
Let us
Withdraw from our truth
Until only his facts we can recall.
Let us

Withdraw from our life
To make his our all in all.

When God isn't there
May that be our call—
Our call to withdraw.

SEVEN

WHEN GOD STOPS
COMING TO CHURCH

If God left, would you notice?

> *Therefore, as I live, declares the Lord GOD,*
> *surely, because you have defiled my sanctuary*
> *with all your detestable things and with all your*
> *abominations, therefore I will withdraw.*
> —EZEKIEL 5:11

In the summer of 2008, I was working as an interim youth minister for a church who had a youth group of about twenty but no one to lead them. Taking up the normal responsibilities of any youth leader, I began teaching Bible class, chatting with kids over coffee, and planning pool parties. Early on in the summer, I was teaching the Sunday-morning teen class when one of my sophomore guys began vomiting in a trash can near the stereotypical "youth room couch." Chalking it up to nothing more than a stomach bug and assuring myself it had nothing to do with the quality of my teaching, I sympathetically instructed him to make his way down to the adult class and inform his mother that he was sick. He was excused and the lesson was completed.

About a month went by, and I began to get to know this young man as more than the kid who got sick during one of my lessons. In fact, he became very dear to me and I to him. Through almost daily discipleship, we began to break through walls and make our way into the inner room of his struggles and sins. As I came to find out, it was neither a stomach bug nor my teaching that had caused him to lose his breakfast a handful of Sundays back. His sickness was a self-imposed mixture of an alcoholic hangover and withdrawals from illegal prescription medication. But what was more shocking than the abuse of drink and substance was the reason he gave me for why he threw up in my class.

His withdrawal symptoms were not due to a lack of supply but a lack of consumption. He had the pills he needed to level out his system but didn't have the time or opportunity to consume them without bringing his misconduct to the attention of his parents before arriving at the church building that morning. He explained that he knew he could have popped them in one of the church's restroom stalls before class started, but he didn't. When I pressed him on why he chose not to self-medicate in some secret corner of the building, he responded boisterously yet blankly, "You can't take drugs in church!"

Would We Even Notice?

My friend made a common assumption about the church building: *God is here.* He assumed that God's presence was tied to a physical religious location. So for him—and for most of us—doing drugs in the same building where God's hanging out is pretty bad. Parents often reinforce this notion about God's presence. When they catch kids misbehaving at church, their rebukes often come with a final phrase: "I can't believe you would do that—and in church of all places!"

For my friend, God's presumed presence at church prohibited his pill popping. The presence of God in his bedroom, at the parties he frequented, or in his car was not enough to stop him from using drugs—but the God who dwelt in the church was. He thought that no matter how absent he was from God without, he could be present to God within. Why? Because he believed that God lives at church.

Masses of churchgoers believe this myth and make the same assumption every Sunday. All over the world, people enter churches with one truth fixed in their minds: God is here. He is waiting to be worshipped, prayed to, admired, lifted up, and honored. The large, picturesque wooden church doors are open so wide they might as well be the arms of God, ever waiting to receive us into his embrace. We think God waits for us in our churches.

But what if one Sunday God decided not to show up to church? Would we even notice? Perhaps we have assumed God's presence in our churches to the point that his absence goes unfelt week in and week out. Maybe this is done out of an attempt to protect ourselves. Like my friend, we self-medicate with our assumptions of God's presence in order to keep us safe from feeling his absence. Perhaps we need to reassess *how* God is present in our churches and *if* he could be absent from them.

Humble Confidence

The people of Israel in the Old Testament believed the same God-lives-in-a-building idea as well—and they had good reason to.

God's presence in a building wasn't a myth to Israel. God himself did dwell in their temple. After David, the psalmist and slayer of Goliath, passed away, his son Solomon took over as king. When Solomon began building the temple for the Lord, God spoke to him and said:

> Concerning this house which you are building, if you will walk in My statutes and execute My ordinances and keep all My commandments by walking in them, then I will carry out My word with you which I spoke to David your father. I will dwell among the sons of Israel, and will not forsake My people Israel. (1 Kings 6:12–13 NASB)

God promised to live with Israel, in their temple, as long as Israel kept its promise to live with God the way he commanded. The temple was a sacred place for the people of Israel. God allowed a special manifestation of his presence to reside in the innermost part of the temple, known as the Holy of Holies.

God was present in the Holy of Holies in a way in which he was absent everywhere else on earth. This was a unique mix of God's relational and visible presence with a light dash of his actual presence thrown in. Therefore, specific rituals had to be followed in order for one priest to enter into that inner room once a year in order to offer a sacrifice.[1] This is why the temple was a holy place— because God actually dwelt there. God gave his presence.

Can you imagine entering a building where the manifest presence of God dwelt? I remember the awe and wonder I felt when I visited the Coliseum in Rome and thought to myself, *This is where Caesar and his people watched the gladiators battle.* The place was eerie and hallowed. But neither a gladiator's boot nor a sandal of Caesar's had stood on that dirt or marble for more than fifteen hundred years. If the reverence and wonderment of an ancient arti-fact can be felt in such a way because of what once occurred there, imagine how mighty the sense of amazement must have been for the Israelite who knew God himself was present in the temple.

Israel was proud of the temple. It was their sign of God's love for them. It was the physical symbol of God's providence and care. It was their beacon of God's presence to themselves and all nations. The temple became a pledge of God's presence to the Israelites. They had a humble confidence that God dwelled there.

This humble confidence is seen clearly in the story of God fill-ing the temple during the reign of Solomon. We have already read the part of the story where God promised Solomon he would dwell in the temple. Well, after the temple was completed, God followed through on that promise in a big way. He miraculously entered the new structure and filled it with his presence like a thick cloud. The encounter inspired Solomon to pray these words:

> But will God indeed dwell on the earth? Behold, heaven and the highest heaven cannot contain you; how much less this house that I have built! Yet have regard to the prayer of your servant and to his plea, . . . that your eyes may be open night and day toward this house, the place of which you have said, "My name shall be there." (1 Kings 8:27–29)

The king was completely blown away that God actually entered into the temple. Solomon knew that God is so immense that not even the highest heaven can hold him (remember the ocean and the Wiffle ball?). So he was floored to think about the reality of God's promise to dwell in the temple.

It's like a fifteen-year-old who is obsessed with her dad's shiny new Corvette. The dad promises to get her a car when she turns sixteen. On her birthday, while she's expecting some cheap starter car, the dad tosses her the keys to his Corvette and says, "It's yours." The daughter would respond like Solomon did: "You're joking, right? This can't be real!"

That is the kind of joyful befuddlement Solomon was expressing when he said, "But will God indeed dwell on the earth?" He was astounded, thrilled, and overwhelmed. His response is a beautiful picture of what humble confidence looks like.

Solomon's understanding of God's presence was much like my understanding of my wedding day. When I saw my wife angelically float down the aisle toward me, shining in her white dress, I said to myself, "Surely this woman cannot be for me!" I knew she was too good for me. I didn't feel proud of my accomplishments in that moment. I was humbled that such a woman would choose me. I was made low but was full of joy.

Solomon expressed the same idea when he said, "Heaven and the highest heaven cannot contain you." He knew he didn't own God's presence, yet God's presence came. This grace of God led to Solomon's humility. Truly understanding the privilege of God's presence produces humility in us.

My wife and I wrote our own vows, and I'm so glad we did. I remember how overwhelmed and grateful I was to hear all the promises my wife made to me during her vows. Her promises gave me confidence that she would be there for me. With every word that spilled from her lips, I was given more assurance that this woman standing in front of me had really chosen me. She really was my wife. She would always be there for me.

Solomon experienced a similar confidence after being so humbled by God's presence. We see this confidence in the request he made. Solomon asked God to have regard for the prayers that would come out of the temple. He asked that God would always keep his

eyes fixed on this house that he had built. Solomon was embold-
ened by the promise of God that said, "My name shall be there." He
trusted in God's faithfulness. The promise of the Almighty made
him sure. This is confidence.

Humble confidence in the presence of God is a bewildered
certainty. We are bewildered by the thought that God could even
possibly be present with us, so we are humbled. But we are certain that he will be present with us because of his promises, so we
are confident. A proper tension between these two keeps us from
growing entitled in our confidence or doubtful in our humility.

How often have you approached God like Solomon? How regularly are you completely befuddled at God's presence and overjoyed
at your chance to commune with him? We have every reason to
respond to God's presence today the same way Solomon did back
in the days of the first temple.

We as Christians can have a humble confidence in God's presence. In fact, we are told in Hebrews 4:16 to "approach God's throne
of grace with confidence" (NIV). We have assurance that God will
be present with us, because he has promised to be. Jesus earned this
presence of God, and our access to the throne of grace, for us. But
we must not allow humble confidence to warp into proud entitlement, especially when it comes to leashing God to a building. For
Jesus did not promise his presence in a place, but to a people.

Proud Entitlement

After many generations of God's temple presence, the people of Israel
began to take that presence for granted. Humility corrupted into
pride, and confidence slipped into entitlement. The temple changed
from a sign of the grace of God's presence to a cage for the guarantee

of God's blessing. As long as Israel had the temple, they had God. If God promised to live in the temple, and they had the temple, then they had the divine presence on a leash. Surely none of the Israelites would have admitted this in such harsh terms, but it was a presumption that lay active in the subconscious of many temple-goers. Humble confidence had turned into proud entitlement.

The way Israel took God's presence for granted is the same way I can quickly start to take my wife for granted. After the wedding decorations were taken down, after the honeymoon had drawn to a close, once her white dress had been in the closet for several years, humble confidence could turn into proud entitlement. I could easily start to think I'm entitled to her loyalty. I could slip into getting comfortable with her trust. I could begin to take her vows as a sure thing and let mine slip.

I exercise proud entitlement when I don't take the extra time to think through my word choice, tone, and heart before speaking with her. My words can be short and sharp. My tone can be rude and distant. My heart can be selfish and cold. The man who stood before his bride so bewildered with humility on his wedding day would never talk to her like that. But the man who forgets the undeserved beauty of his bride easily forgets to speak to her with befuddled appreciation.

We do the same thing with God's presence. When we assume that God's presence is always on our side, we allow entitlement to erode our thankfulness, commitment, and holiness. When his promises cease to amaze us, his presence will cease to humble us. When his assurances begin to make us entitled instead of confident, we will become presumptuous instead of thankful. Humility brings obedience and gratefulness. Pride brings apathy and demand for privilege.

Israel began to forget the "wedding vows" Solomon took in

1 Kings. They not only forgot them but did the exact opposite. Instead of recognizing that they could not contain God, they began to believe that God was detained in the temple. Instead of God's promises leading them to humility, God's promises led them to entitlement. And instead of pledging their lives to God in light of such an amazing commitment, Israel lived their lives however they wanted. They cheated in their businesses, exploited the poor, defrauded the widows, and murdered the innocent.

Much like my wife would be if I treated her like this, God was deeply hurt and sent the prophet Jeremiah to express his pain. "What fault did your ancestors find in me, that they strayed so far from me? . . . The priests did not ask, 'Where is the LORD?' Those who deal with the law did not know me" (Jer. 2:5, 8 NIV). God was speaking like a wounded lover. "What's so wrong with me? Am I not good enough for you anymore? Why did you leave me?" The leaders of the temple stopped asking where God was and just assumed he was there. Such proud entitlement offended God and led to absence.[2]

God was hurt that the priests did not ask, "Where is the Lord?" He was hurt because apparently he had withdrawn his presence from the temple and no one even noticed.[3] Could you imagine a husband coming home and not noticing whether his wife was there or not? Could you imagine a bride walking down the aisle, not realizing that her groom is not waiting for her at the altar? But Israel was going into the temple without recognizing that God was absent. Israel forgot their God. They were going about religion without God. They were claiming presence, but all they had was absence. They didn't know that God had left the building.[4]

This raises the question, Does God withdraw from our church buildings today? When we presume upon his presence, act entitled in our position, and refuse to reform our actions in response to his grace, does he become absent in our worship services as he became absent to Israel's temple? And if he did, would we even realize he was gone?

This is nearly impossible to comment on in broad strokes. So instead, let us hear how God warned the Israelites through Jeremiah, letting each of us inspect our hearts to see if we are coming to God in humble confidence or proud entitlement.

The Temple Sermon

In response to such a horrible misuse of the temple, God sent Jeremiah to stand outside of its gates and preach. This story is found in Jeremiah 7 and is known as the temple sermon. His message to the people of Israel was that God's presence was not bound by the temple, nor were the people of Israel safe just by being present inside of it. The temple-goers believed they could live their lives any way they saw fit, as long as they went to temple like good Jewish men and women. They would come to the temple, bring their sacrifices, and hold their heads high because they believed God was inside and was required to accept them.

This would be like an alcoholic who feels he's earned a night of binge drinking because he attended an AA meeting. It would be like a father thinking he could take a few years off from parenting because he took his kids to Disney World. It would be like a smoker wearing a nicotine patch so that she could smoke two packs a day. Israel's assumption of God's presence in the temple led to a sense of entitlement that freed them up to live any way they wanted. The days of humble confidence were over.

So Jeremiah stood outside the temple and preached his message. There are three statements Jeremiah made that I would like us to focus on. The first two were a form of mockery. In these, Jeremiah quoted some of the things people said in the temple and turned them on their heads. The two statements of mockery are "This is the temple of the LORD" (v. 4 NIV) and "We are safe" (v. 10 NIV).

The final statement I want us to zoom in on may be familiar to you because Jesus quoted it himself: "Has this house, which bears my Name, become a den of robbers to you?" (v. 11 NIV). We will look at each of these briefly and see what God has to say to us when our humble confidence in his presence turns into proud entitlement.

"This Is the Temple of the LORD"

While Jeremiah was standing outside the temple, preaching his sermon, he began to mock one of the songs that the people sang inside the sanctuary walls: "Do not trust in deceptive words and say, 'This is the temple of the LORD, the temple of the LORD, the temple of the LORD!'" (Jer. 7:4 NIV). Biblical scholar Samuel Terrien argued that this was most likely a chanted phrase, which was repeated over and over again by the people inside the temple like a hymn or a song.[5] Instead of actually praising God, they were praising their privilege as God's people and their sacred space as God's home. It was religious self-speak. Their own worship songs were telling them lies.

Like Israel, we have fallen victim to the idea that just because a church building bears God's name, it means that it must bear his presence. We approach our Sunday mornings like a scheduled face-to-face with the Almighty. We structure our church services to create an experience or an ecstatic encounter. We have assigned the presence of God to goose bumps and good feelings.

Many of our modern worship songs don't declare the works and glory of God, but proclaim or request an experience with God.

"You are here! God is moving! Let fire fall!" Worship is focused on tying God down and lifting worshippers up.

Six days a week God may feel absent or far off, but on our structured Sundays he feels present and close by. We have confused God's presence with a type of feeling or emotion. We must be careful not to let our worship songs and Sunday assumptions become our manipulative mantra. We must not let the precious worship of our God turn into self-deception.

"We Are Safe"

Jeremiah continued his sermon with more mockery. He took aim at another message that was regularly proclaimed in the temple: "We are safe." The priests of Jeremiah's day were guilty of preaching this message of false safety. Jeremiah accused them of treating the people's wound as if it were not fatal when it actually was extremely deadly: "They dress the wound of my people as though it were not serious. 'Peace, peace,' they say, when there is no peace" (6:14 NIV).

Unrepentant, sin-loving people were coming into the temple and leaving unchanged, because all the priests would tell them was, "You are safe." It was like they were putting a Band-Aid on a bullet wound. No one was the least concerned with the condition of their souls while in the temple because, according to the priests, neither was God. Their association with the temple created a false sense of peace between them and their God.

Jeremiah summed up this thought well by mocking the speech of the temple leaders. God said through Jeremiah, "Will you steal and murder, commit adultery and perjury, burn incense to Baal and follow other gods you have not known, and then come and stand before me in this house, which bears my Name, and say, 'We are safe'—safe to do all these detestable things?" (7:9–10 NIV).

Jeremiah's response to the priest's false promises of safety was to point out their sins. Whereas the priests were sweeping sin under the rug, refusing to recognize it at all, Jeremiah shone a huge light on it and called them out by name. Many churches today perform the same sweeping motion as the priests of Jeremiah's day. They refuse to call sin by name, preferring instead to only speak of love, grace, and forgiveness. "Safe" is far more often on many preachers' lips than "Repent!"

Our presumptions of presence lead to presumptions of safety. If God is always showing up at our churches, conferences, and worship nights, even though our lives and the lives of those around us are actually far from God, then maybe our lives aren't all that bad. If God is present where I am present, what do I have to worry about? At this point, entitlement turns God's presence into a static idol. Jeremiah made this point exceedingly clear when he called the temple "a den of robbers."

"A Den of Robbers"

You may be familiar with the story of Ali Baba and the Forty Thieves. This band of thieves, led by their captain, went about pillaging and looting houses and towns in the most dastardly ways. Once their ransacking was completed and their beasts of burden loaded to capacity, they would head back to their now infamous cave. The company would stand at the hidden mouth of the cavern until the captain's voice rang out the secret password, "Open Sesame!" At the sound of the words, the secret doors would open and the thieves would conceal themselves inside, safe from the world with their plunder.

The den was a hideout for the robbers. It was a place into which they could escape from all the possible repercussions earned by their monstrous deeds. They needed only speak the magic words and they would be shut inside the protective walls of their cave. They were safe, safe to continue all their detestable deeds.

This is the idea God communicated through Jeremiah when he stood outside the temple in Israel and said, "Has this house, which is called by my name, become a den of robbers in your eyes?" (7:11). God was accusing his people of living lives of sin while using the temple as their moral hiding place.

The same could be said of the way we treat our churches. We go about our lives as we wish, pillaging like the forty thieves. When our six days of selfish living are complete and we have the treasures earned by sin wrapped up in sacks upon our backs, we make our way to church. Speaking the secret words of our songs, prayers, and happy greetings, we open the doors to the "presence of God" with our religious "Open Sesame!" The doors of the auditorium shut behind us, and we decide we are safe. We believe we are absolved in an hour and then head back out into the villages for more pillaging.

God's presence cannot be seen as a license for sin. Meeting with God on Sunday should not entitle us to live however we want, but should transform us to live however he wants. We are not safe from God's justice just because we go to church.

Singing enthusiastically at church does not allow us to speak angrily with others at home. Taking notes during the sermon does not open the door for us to cook the books at our job. Putting a generous check in the offering plate does not give us the right to cheat on our taxes. Closing our eyes tightly during prayer does not make it okay for us to open them to look at pornography. Assuming God's presence at church must not give us a holy excuse to do whatever we want.

Jesus Clears the Temple

When Jesus used the phrase "den of robbers," he was also at the temple. And, like Jeremiah, his presence was not a welcome or agreeable one either. Matthew 21:12–13 records what happened:

> Jesus entered the temple courts and drove out all who were buying and selling there. He overturned the tables of the moneychangers and the benches of those selling doves. "It is written," he said to them, "'My house will be called a house of prayer,' but you are making it 'a den of robbers.'" (NIV)

Many have understood this story as Jesus' indictment against buying and selling goods in the house of God, but this is not the chief meaning of Jesus' actions. After all, a den of robbers is not where the robbing is done, but where you hide out after the crime has been committed.

The buying of sacrifices in the temple couldn't be what caused Jesus to drive out the moneychangers. This is because the people of Israel were actually commanded to buy their sacrifices at the temple if the journey was too long for them to make with their animals.[6] In fact, N. T. Wright argued that these service providers could be seen as relatively good, as they helped carry out the function of the temple. Wright explained that without the tax taken upon entry, support for daily sacrifices wouldn't have been supplied. Without the correct form of currency, temple-goers couldn't purchase animals. Without animals, sacrifices would be nonexistent. Without sacrifices, the temple would have lost its reason for existing.

Jesus was not behaving like a radical social activist, marching on the temple to reform its economic practices. He was making a prophetic demonstration by causing a short and abrupt cessation of temple activities. By causing a disruption in the flow of sacrifices, Jesus was saying that the ultimate sacrifice for sin was here and that after he tore down the temple of his body on the cross, no further sacrifices in the temple would ever be necessary again. Jesus set himself up as the new temple, the ultimate sacrifice, and the ultimate place of God's presence.[7]

When Jesus mentioned the den of robbers from Jeremiah, he wasn't alluding to the money changers. Jesus was talking about the entire temple system. By quoting Jeremiah's temple sermon, Jesus knew his listeners would understand that he was condemning them for the same practices as their forefathers.

Jesus was saying that people were still assuming God's presence as a means of their entitlement. They were killing animals for sin, but they were not killing sin in their own lives. They were honoring the assumed presence of God in the temple but ignoring the presence of God in their daily lives. The temple was still a den of robbers.

The ultimate irony of the situation is that when Jesus entered the temple, God was present inside of it in a new way. No longer was he just present in the Holy of Holies, to be visited once a year. He was now physically present in the general courts, where everyone could see him. God was in the temple, and he was setting up new ground rules for his presence.

No longer would people need to sacrifice animals to stand before God, because Jesus would be their sacrifice once and for all. God would no longer be sequestered off behind a veil in the Holy of Holies; he would stand among the people and live with them. God was present in a new way. Jesus would be the sacrifice for all the detestable deeds of Israel from Jeremiah's day, all the horrible sins of humanity since the fall of Adam and Eve, and every single transgression that would be committed by you and me in the years to come. God is now present with his people through Jesus Christ.

We have a better promise than Israel regarding God's presence. God promised to be present to Israel if they remained faithful to the Law. As long as Israel did everything God commanded, God would be present with his people. Of course, as we have seen, Israel was incapable of doing that. So God's presence was taken from them.

But our promise is not based on our goodness, righteousness, or behavior. God is present with us because of the perfect work of Jesus. How much more confidence can we have to come boldly before the throne of grace? And how much more susceptible are we to the pitfall of proud entitlement?

The apostle Paul recognized this pitfall and addressed it in Romans 6:1. He asked the hypothetical question to his readers, "Shall we go on sinning so that grace may increase?" (NIV). Paul was asking, since we are saved by Jesus' perfect blood, why shouldn't we live however we want? If we are safe in Jesus, aren't we safe to do all the detestable things we want? As our sin grows, doesn't grace grow? But Paul answered his own question in verse 2: "By no means!" (NIV). We must not fall into the same sin as Israel did when they made the temple a den of robbers. Grace, like God's presence, must change us.

In fact, the more we long for God's presence, the more we will long to kill sin and to obey his commands. Because just as Israel's sin drove God away from them, our obedience of God draws us deeper into his presence. Author and theologian David Murray put it this way: "Like Israel, we are *redeemed* by mercy, brought into a living *relationship* with Jesus, for which we show our gratitude by obeying His *rules*, which He in turn also graciously *rewards* with more of His presence. Loving obedience brings Jesus into the soul and the soul to Jesus."[8]

Perhaps this promise is best summed up in Scripture: "Whoever has my commandments and keeps them, he it is who loves me. And he who loves me will be loved by my Father, and I will love him and manifest myself to him."[9] Our desire for God's presence leads us to a radical desire for holy living.

Jeremiah himself is extremely helpful at this point (how kind of God to prescribe us the remedy to absence in a book that so often diagnoses it). Within the temple sermon itself, God says this through Jeremiah: "For if you truly amend your ways and your deeds, if you truly execute justice one with another, if you do not oppress the sojourner, the fatherless, or the widow, or shed innocent blood in this place, and if you do not go after other gods to your own harm, then I will let you dwell in this place" (7:5–7). Sin separates us from God. Repent! Return to God and he will return to you. Or as James says, "Draw near to God, and he will draw near to you" (4:8).

So Is God Ever at Church with Me?

You may be asking at this point, *So how do I know if God is present in my church? How do I keep myself humbly confident without becoming proudly entitled?* The answer lies in the knowledge that God's presence relates to us as individuals and corporately, not to a building.

When Jesus came to the temple, he said, "Do you see these great buildings? There will not be left here one stone upon another that will not be thrown down" (Mark 13:2). Jesus was saying that the temple was soon to be no more. Jesus made clear the reason for the destruction of the temple when he said, "I tell you, something greater than the temple is here" (Matt. 12:6). The thing that was greater than the temple was Jesus himself.

After Jesus' death and resurrection, the temple would pass away because the sacrifices it continually offered on behalf of sin were now, once and for all, dealt with in the blood of Christ. The need to work and toil over salvation had been done away with. There was no longer a need for a structure to exist that dealt with humanity's sins. The cross was the only structure that would ever be needed.

But what about the presence of God that dwelt in the temple? What happened to it? Where is it now? You may remember that when Jesus was crucified, the veil, which separated the Holy of Holies from the rest of the temple, was torn in two. This revealed that the temple was no longer needed to mediate between God and man. Jesus was now our perfect pathway into God's presence. God does not dwell in places, but in people. As Paul said in 1 Corinthians 6:19, "Do you not know that your body is a temple of the Holy Spirit within you, whom you have from God?" God no longer dwells *among* his people, as he did in the Old Testament and in the old temple. God now dwells *within* his people.[10]

There is a special, relational manifestation of God's presence now dwelling inside every Christian. He made no such covenant or promise with a building, church, artifact, statue, altar, or specific denomination. God does not live in buildings. "The Most High does not dwell in houses made by hands, as the prophet says, 'Heaven is my throne, and the earth is my footstool. What kind of house will you build for me, says the Lord, or what is the place of my rest? Did not my hand make all these things?'" (Acts 7:48–50).

God is generally present with every part of creation but relationally present with every single Christian. If you are a Christian, God is relationally present with you in a way that he is specifically absent from non-Christians. Christians are living temples of the Holy Spirit and have been given a new mode of God's presence that the rest of the world does not have.

God is not caged for our amusement or our sin's appeasement. Walking into a church is not synonymous with walking into the presence of God. Sunday mornings are not magic lamps we rub that summon the presence of God like a genie. Nor are our songs and prayers like pagan incantations or séances that beckon him to come near us. Our churches do not guarantee the presence of God like we may want them to. And even the smallest amount of this type of thinking can lead to dangerous outcomes. Just like they did with the people of Jeremiah's day in the old temple.

Jesus is our only guarantee of God's presence. We must understand that since God dwells in Christians, like movable temples, when we come together to worship we form a huge spiritual building. This structure cannot be seen, but it is massive—and God dwells inside of our praises (Ps. 22:3). We are experiencing a collective lifting up of the Lord whenever we come together en masse as Christians. This does not form some kind of holy magnet that pulls God over. God traveled with us to church!

So if you need to answer the question, Is God present at my church? ask yourself the question, *Are there Christians at my church?*[11] If there are Christians, then there is Christ. First John 4:12 juxtaposes God's actual and visible absence with his special, relational presence: "No one has ever seen God; if we love one another, God abides in us and his love is perfected in us."

It's true that no one has seen God. But as the church loves one another, God abides in us, and we can see and experience Christ in one another. We are moving temples. If you need to answer the question, *How do I keep myself humbly confident without becoming proudly entitled?* remember what the presence of God cost. God's presence in us cost the very life of God incarnate. Jesus suffered on the cross so that we may sing confidently in God's presence on Sunday. If we keep the cross at the center of our vision, pride and entitlement will not be able to find a foothold.

EIGHT

WHERE TWO OR THREE ARE GATHERED

Where is God in worship?

It was Solomon who built a house for him.
Yet the Most High does not dwell in houses
made by hands, as the prophet says,

"'Heaven is my throne,
and the earth is my footstool.
What kind of house will you build for me,
says the Lord,
or what is the place of my rest?
Did not my hand make all these things?'"
—ACTS 7:47–50

Depending on your age or your fascination with nostalgic board games, you may or may not have heard of Mouse

Trap. Mouse Trap is a board game, first released in 1963, based around a series of chain reactions. As the game progresses, you and the other players build an elaborate plastic machine that ends in dropping an elevated red cage down upon a tiny mouse character standing atop a wheel of cheese.

I absolutely loved this game as a kid, but you had to make sure that all the mechanisms were lined up exactly right or the inter-weaving reactions would not trigger as they were supposed to. The machine started by cranking a few plastic gears that tightened up a rubber band, which was anchored to a leveraged stop sign. Once the stop sign whipped back from the tension, the trap was set in motion. A boot kicked a marble down a terraced slope, and a red slide moved the ball to the bottom of a pole that triggered another ball to fall from a great height into a bathtub. The bathtub emptied out onto a diving board, which flipped a green diver into a small yellow pool. The vibrations of the diver landing in the pool shook the serrated pole that held the red trap, causing it to fall.

If everything was lined up perfectly, the game worked like it was supposed to. However, if one tiny thing was out of line or if one of the balls lost momentum during its route, the whole system shut down into a disappointing standstill.

I think many of us, consciously or unconsciously, view God's presence in worship in a similar way. If the worship team chooses the right song, if the good singer is leading, if the music is at the proper volume, if the lights are set just right, and if we happen to be particularly in tune that Sunday morning, then we get to experi-ence God. But if one thing gets out of line, all is lost. I realize this is a farcical and caricatured way to look at how we approach worship, but there is a measure of truth in it. We believe that certain things have to be in place for God to show up.

Worship has become about presence. We want to conjure up the visible, tangible presence of God. Worship has become about aligning all our mechanisms just right so that we can trap the mouse in its cage. Unfortunately for us, the mouse we are trying to trap is the almighty God, and no cage can contain him—not even church-shaped ones.

Where Two or More Are Gathered

One of the "mechanisms" most commonly used to get the mouse in the cage, at least in our minds, is the regularly quoted verse from Matthew 18:20: "Where two or three gather in my name, there am I with them" (NIV). This verse is often used as an assurance of God's presence within a gathering of Christians. I have heard it used to sanction small group Bible studies, guarantee the presence of God at church services, and declare God's nearness at large conferences. I've even misused this verse in my own writing (for which I now apologize).[1] Unfortunately, this verse is not talking about God's presence at all.

In Matthew 18:15–20, Jesus is instructing his disciples concerning what to do when someone in the church is found in sin. The first step is for one person to go and confront the sinner with their sin just between the two of them. If they will not listen, the next step is to confront them with one or two others so that "every matter may be established by the testimony of two or three witnesses" (v. 16 NIV; cf. Deut. 19:15).

The idea of having two or three witnesses comes from the Old Testament law. The law required at least two or three witnesses to a crime in order for certain punishments to be carried out.[2] This is very similar to the jury boxes and witness stands of our courtrooms today. Therefore, in the church, if the sinner will not repent after having been confronted by two or three witnesses, then their sin is to be told to the congregation. After all this, if the sinner still will not change their ways, they are to be put out of fellowship.

Jesus continues to explain that whatever they decide in the churches he will agree with in heaven. This is not to say that Jesus bends to our will, but quite the opposite. The church is supposed to be the physical reflection of a spiritual reality. The reality of how God is relating to this sinner in heaven is to be expressed physically on earth. The community of the church is supposed to be a window into the community of heaven. That is why Jesus finally says, "Where two or three gather in my name, there am I with them."

This promise is about Jesus' approval of church authority. Jesus is saying that he will agree with a church's choice to excommunicate a sinner if two or three stand as a witness against him. He is with them in their decision.

For many people, realizing that this verse doesn't mean what they originally thought can feel like something precious has been taken away from them. And though I don't want to press the point further than it needs to be, I think it is important to point out that we may have other false ideas about God's presence in worship that need to be debunked.

Have we actually tested our assumptions about how God's presence relates to worship? Have we thoroughly examined the claims we make about God dwelling in our praises? Have we searched deep into the scriptures we regularly use to talk about God showing up in our gatherings, like Matthew 18:20? Perhaps we need to begin by reevaluating what the purpose of God's presence is.

Why Would God Want to Be Present?

We talk a lot about God "showing up" in our churches, but have we ever stopped to ask why God would want to show up in the first place? What lies in the heart of God that moves him to be present with us? Why is God's presence even an option at all? What is the point of presence? We often think God's presence is about us, but it is not. We believe that God comes near to us because he loves us so much. He does love us more than we can know, but that is not the chief reason for his presence.

God is present with us because his presence is the greatest thing in all existence. God is present because he gives good gifts. God gives us himself because he is the best gift. The presence of God is all about us receiving the greatest treasure in the universe so that we may give praise to the greatest treasure in the universe. Presence is possible because God most wants to give us himself.

Perhaps no one has explained this better than preacher and theologian John Piper in his book *Desiring God*. He began by explaining that God most loves God.

> God would be unrighteous (just as we would) if He valued any-
> thing more than what is supremely valuable. But He Himself
> is supremely valuable. If He did not take infinite delight in the
> worth of His own glory, He would be unrighteous. For it is right
> to take delight in a person in proportion to the excellence of that
> person's glory.[3]

If God did not love himself more than anything else, he would be committing idolatry and proclaiming that there is something better than himself. Piper continued, "If God should turn away from Himself as the Source of infinite joy, He would cease to be God. He would deny the infinite worth of His own glory. He would imply that there is something more valuable outside Himself. He would commit idolatry."[4] In everything God does, he must seek to give himself glory and proclaim his own ultimate worth.

Therefore, God's presence cannot be mainly or preeminently

about us. God's presence is about God. God's love for us is about God's love for himself. Listen to this further explanation by Piper:

> Consider this question: In view of God's infinite power and wisdom and beauty, what would His love for a human being involve? Or to put it another way: What could God give us to enjoy that would prove Him most loving? There is only one possible answer: *Himself!* If He withholds Himself from our contemplation and companionship, no matter what else He gives us, He is not loving.[5]

God is present with us not just because he loves us. His presence with us is *how* he loves us. When God becomes present with us, he gives us the most valuable gift in the universe: himself. In so doing, God secures our praise for the most valuable being in existence: God. We do not worship the feelings God's presence gives us. We do not worship the joy God's presence gives us. We do not worship the glory of God's presence. We worship God alone, and the rest follows.

Do you want to experience God in worship in the way he intended? Then praise that which is most praiseworthy and you will be swept up in God's mighty and unstoppable plan to give the most worth to the most worthy. As Piper summarized, "God's pursuit of praise from us and our pursuit of pleasure in Him are the same pursuit."[6]

This redefines the presence of God from the ground up. The presence of God is not about us. It is about God. God draws near to us to give himself glory through us. Because when we find ourselves glorifying him alone, we will be the most satisfied, the most loved, and the most joyful. He is the best gift that could ever be given. This forces the presence of God out of a self-serving, self-focused endeavor. We no longer seek the presence of God because we want to feel something, prove something, or absolve ourselves of something.

We draw near to God because we want to give him glory. For in so doing we will find our highest pleasure on this earth.

Coincidentally, understanding that God most wants to give us himself flips the divine motive for presence on its head. Many of us believe that God draws near to us because of something in us. He draws near to me because I am desirable. He wants to be present with me because I am lovable to him. These statements are not fully true. God does love us. But God draws near to us because he is desirous of his glory for the sake of our pleasure. God longs to be present with us because he is the most lovable being in all existence, and he loves us so much that he wants us to share in that love.

God's presence is about God's glory. God drawing near is about God being lifted up. God comes down so that he may be exalted high. The presence of God can be defined as God giving us himself for his greatest glory and our greatest satisfaction. God gives us more of himself so we can make the most out of him. The presence of God is about the glory of God.

Worship and Presence

With this better understanding of presence now in our minds, let's take a look at how God's presence relates to worship. The best place to begin a discussion about God's presence and absence in worship is with an understanding of what worship is and is not.

Worship is all about God. Worship reveres God with fear and wonder, submits to God, pays him homage, responds to his grace, and obeys his will. Worship is about ascribing worth to the most worthy. Worship is about giving honor to the most honorable. Worship is about exalting the only exalted one. But we have increasingly made worship about us.

Much of modern worship is designed to fulfill a task that is completely opposite to its purpose. Worship is about exalting God, which means lifting him up. However, our worship has become centered around bringing God down, that is to say beckoning his presence to fall upon us and be among us. The purpose of worship is to make God the center, yet we have hijacked worship so that we may put ourselves at the center. It is our experience, not God's excellence, that is receiving the most attention. It is our goose bumps, not the gospel, that is attracting the most focus. Worship is no longer about worship; it is about experience.

It is hard to attend a contemporary worship service without immediately running into multiple references to ourselves, our emotions, our experience, our ability to see God in this place, or our desire for him to come down among us. While desiring the presence of God is not a bad thing at all (in fact, this entire book is about how we long to be more present with God than we are), we must be careful not to steal worship away from God for the sake of drawing attention to our needs, desires, and emotions. Worship is all about God. But how can we put God back into the center of worship?

One way you can begin to change your habits in worship is to be more aware of what you are singing. Don't just sing the words because they pop up on a screen. Consider their meaning, their truth, and whether you believe them.[7] As you do this, you will begin to find lines in certain songs that you don't agree with. The good news is that worship is not all about the words you sing. Worship is also about the state of your heart when you go to praise God.[8]

So you can sing some of the words that used to put you at the center of worship but change the purpose behind why you choose to sing them in your heart. Consider a few types of common lines you may have heard some variation of in your worship service.

We regularly sing about how God is present with us in worship. "God is in this place," "I feel you near," and "I see your face" are all types of things that many worshippers sing on a Sunday morning. But what do we mean when we sing about God being present and seeing him in our churches? Do we mean that God is generally present? Of course he is! God is present everywhere. We would even be correct in saying that God is relationally present in most of the people with whom we are worshipping because we are all Christians in whom the Holy Spirit lives.

God is present in worship. In fact, Hebrews 2:12 says that Jesus leads us in worship to the Father. John Calvin, in commenting on this passage in Hebrews, wrote, "Christ . . . is the chief Conductor of our hymns."[9]

We must be careful, however, not to make our claims on God's presence too huge or too hasty. When we sing about God's presence in worship, are we claiming that he is present in a way that he has not promised to be? Have we summoned him down to us in worship or lifted him up? Even when we are worshipping God, we must be careful not to step beyond the scope of God's promised presence in our churches.

Furthermore, we can be too hasty in our declaration that God is here. Do we sing that he is in this place as a response to God showing up in a big way? Or is it played because it is the next song on the set list? Would the worship band sing the song anyway if God wasn't present in a special or manifest way? Do we stop and ask, "Where is the Lord?" like the priests from Jeremiah refused to do, or do we trudge on ahead, assuming that if we name it we can claim it? There is a sense of proud entitlement in some of our worship songs that claim God's presence as a given.

Another regular idea that makes its way into worship is that of God's glory being revealed among us. We claim to see his glory, feel his glory, and taste his glory. While it is true that we can "taste and see that the LORD is good" (Ps. 34:8), are we claiming to see that which God said would kill Moses? He could not stand in the full presence of God's glory and live, and neither can we.

God is holy; we cannot stand in his actual presence—at least not in this life. I completely understand the desire to sing of standing in God's glory. It is the feeling I experienced so acutely in the plastic-bag cave of Red 2. But we are not yet where we can only imagine. We are absent from God in the way we most desire.

But there is a great heart behind lines and songs like these. They reveal a powerful longing in our hearts. We long to have more of God than we have now. We want to feel God's presence so we sing that we already do. We want to stand in God's glory so we claim that we already are. We want to look into God's face so we proclaim that we already can. But this is the wrong approach. Instead, let us sing that we want to feel his presence, that we long to stand in his glory, that we yearn to see his face.

When songs like these come up on a Sunday morning, you can still sing them, but with a new point of view. We can claim that God is here, out of our humble confidence that he has promised to dwell with us. And we can even say that we are standing in his glory, if we remember that his immense and sustaining general presence, his Spirit in our brothers and sisters, and the gospel message soon to be proclaimed from the pulpit are all vessels of the glory of God. Let songs such as these awaken our longing and our desire for God's presence instead of encouraging our entitlement. After all, we must remember that though the church is part of God's plan for unfolding his presence into the world, it is not the end. God's presence, even in the church, is limited.[10] We look for and long for God's actual face-to-face presence. This is not the end.

Enjoying God in Worship

While we must never forget that worship is mainly about ascribing worth to God, worship is also about enjoying God. Back in 1646, theologians from the Church of England and the Church of Scotland came together at the Westminster Assembly in London. This assembly was held in order that these two Christian groups might have greater unity through a shared confession of faith—that is, a carefully written document that outlines what a certain group believes.

People have been trying to figure out what the meaning and purpose of life is for centuries. Well, I believe the first line of the Westminster Confession says it almost perfectly. The confession opens with these words, "Man's chief end is to glorify God, and to enjoy him forever." The meaning of life is twofold: glorify God and enjoy him forever. These two ideas go hand in hand. One leads to the other. In fact, John Piper went so far as to revise this statement to read, "The chief end of man is to glorify God *by* enjoying him forever."[11]

We cannot truly enjoy God without giving him glory. And we cannot truly give God glory without enjoying him. Only when we place God in the highest place can we enjoy him with the greatest joy.

It's like when you get together with a bunch of friends to watch a sporting event, like a football game, or a television show, like *The Bachelorette*. You have most likely been to a viewing party for a game, show, or movie at a friend's house and everyone was talking over the program, standing in front of the set, and giving no heed to what you all actually got together to enjoy. Every now and then someone would notice that your team scored a touchdown or that your favorite bachelor received a rose. Everyone lightly clapped and then moved on with their conversation. The moment really wasn't enjoyed.

But you have probably also been to a viewing party where everyone was glued to the television. The volume was loud enough for everyone to hear. The show was given top billing at the party. You didn't just passively cheer when a touchdown was scored. You sounded off yard lines as the running back hurtled toward the end zone. Everyone was enjoying the show far more, because it had been put in its proper place.

In the same way, God can only be enjoyed when he is placed in his proper place, which is above all else. That is what it means to glorify him. We lift God up in worship not because he is low and needs our lifting, but because we elevate him in our own hearts and minds as we sing. We make him the greatest and most satisfying thing in our lives. We praise him and him alone. This is the part of the worship experience that is about us. We lift God up in our hearts and, by doing so, experience our greatest joy in him.

When we ascribe to God his proper place, high above all else, then we can truly enjoy him. When we go into worship with our minds set on glorifying God and placing him above everything, our enjoyment of him will follow like a mighty wave about to crash down on all the dry places of our souls. Make your worship about God, and he will satisfy you. Worship is not a means to an end; it is an end in itself. We worship God because he is worthy of worship. We sing to him because he, and he alone, deserves our praise. We worship because our souls long for satisfaction, and that satisfaction is found in God. After all, the only reason we can rejoice in God is because he first is rejoicing over us.[12] The joy we experience in worship is reciprocal joy.

Don't make worship about conjuring presence or catching the

mouse in its trap. Make presence about lifting God up so high above you that his presence becomes impossible. Then, when he is the focus of your praises and elevated far above you, in his proper place of worship, he will satisfy you and fill you with joy more abiding than any manufactured or machined trap of presence. Worship's chief end is to glorify God. By glorifying him in worship we will enjoy him in it as we never have before. The psalmist said it best in Psalm 16:11: "In your presence there is fullness of joy; at your right hand are pleasures forevermore."

AFFLICTION,
ABANDONMENT, AND ABSENCE

Where Is God in Suffering?

Where is God in suffering?

Perhaps a more important question is
Where would you want him to be?

Because, so often, we
Shove him to one of two extremes.

Either he
Is the vengeful cause behind all our pain,
Or he is nowhere to be seen.

But God cannot be
The moral agent, completely
Responsible for every

Obstacle that causes us grief.
Because if God forced sinners to sin
He would not be
Perfect, pure and holy.

But God does not have to force sinners to sin,
Because sinners just sin.
And this is where the other extreme begins.
For if, from head to toe,
People are bad on the whole
Then God need not cause our pain or be in control.
For we would contrive our own demise
Without God ever having to play a role.

But this roll of thought
Is half true and half not.
Because man is totally depraved—
From the core he rots.
But that does not mean God totally stays
Out of mankind's malicious ways.

For over this world is some common grace.

God is in control and will not let our depravity reign.
So he is not some absentee
Who, on the banks of this world, declared bankruptcy.
No!
God is still in control in the midst of all our misery.

So when asked again,
"Where is God in our suffering?"

I'll respond,
"Where would you want him to be?"

For he
Did not choose
Pain as
His malicious plan
Nor did he simply just
Wash his hands.

So
Where is God
In all of our agony?

He is right where you'd want him to be.

Sinners sin and cause pain,
But God's plan has never changed.

Depraved people hurt people,
But God's control has never waned.

For I am not okay
With implicating
God with sin's wage.

But neither would I want
To live in a world
Where God did not control
Every gunshot's blast or tornado's twirl.

For even our sin,
Even our hate,
Even our violence,
Even our rage,
Even our racism,
Even our wars,
Even our abortions,
Even our morgues,

Are all organized by and ordained for
Our God who cannot be blamed for our mistakes
But wouldn't dream of abandoning us in this state.

So where is God in our suffering?
He's right where you'd want him to be.
On the cross to intervene
And take the pain of our suffering.

NINE

PRESENCE IN SUFFERING

Is God present when we suffer?

How long, O Lord? Will you forget me forever?
How long will you hide your face from me?
How long must I take counsel in my soul
and have sorrow in my heart all the day?
How long shall my enemy be exalted over me?
—Psalm 13:1–2

In January 2015, I was spending a week in England, working with a friend on an evangelistic campaign for British schools. One morning, while I was making tea in an electric kettle, the power in the house in which I was staying went out. My host was out for the day on business, so I was alone. It was a very old and very large home on a very cold and very wet day in a very small and very remote village.

As all the radiators stopped purring with heat, the old

manor quickly went from drafty to refrigerated. With two blankets wrapped around me like an inconvenient cape, I went hunting for the fuse box. After nearly an hour of searching, I couldn't find the fuse box, but I did stumble upon my own frustration.

All I wanted to do was answer e-mails, but the Internet was down. All I wanted to do was work on some writing projects, but my computer was dead. All I wanted to do was read, but it was too cold to focus. I began pacing through the house praying for God to fix the problem. "Just do this one thing for me. I know this is easily in your power. Please show yourself!"

A little melodramatic and first world of me, I know, but I think it shows how quickly we tend to turn things around on God when they go wrong. We all go through trials, whether stupid and small or horrible and huge. And when God doesn't immediately show himself, we assume he is absent.

My little episode in that English manor was not a form of suffering. It was, at most, an inconvenience. Those who have experienced true suffering know how quickly the human mind runs to assumptions of God's absence and abandonment. But, as we will uncover in this chapter, God is not absent in suffering; he is very present and active inside of it. In fact, God regularly uses suffering to shape us. In our suffering, God prepares us for himself. In our hardships, God prepares us for his presence. One of my favorite examples of how pain prepares us for presence is found in the book *The Great Divorce* by C. S. Lewis.

Lewis painted a fictional picture of the afterlife in which those who dwell in hell can take a flying bus up into heaven. You may think this would be a violation of the exclusivity of heaven, but no one from hell really ever wants to stay. There are many reasons for this, but the first reason heaven doesn't quite suit the hellish visitors hits them right when they step out of the bus.

The grass of heaven cuts their feet. Those new to the heavenly realm are but a shadow in this land of permanency. They are frail, paper-like, and thin amid the heavenly world that is solid, heavy, and thick. The main character fears that it might soon begin to rain, which would surely be like a barrage of bullets from the skies that would rip him to shreds. He cannot make the grass bend under his feet, nor can he pluck a daisy from the ground since it seems to him to be as heavy as a sack of coal.

The visitors are ill-prepared for the weight of this new world. However, as the main character begins to walk about the place, his feet start to grow slightly more solid the more they are cut. The tearing of his feet produces in him the ability to stand upon the blades of grass. Like scar tissue, the longer the visitors stay in heaven, the more resilient to its weight they become. The residents in the land, those who live in heaven, are called "solid people." The grass effortlessly presses into the damp soil beneath their feet because they have been prepared for such a world.

Suffering toughens up our skin. We suffer now so we will not suffer later. Through many trials we must enter the kingdom of heaven.[1] Suffering is a sign of sanctification, which is the lifelong process of becoming more like Christ. The burden of your load may feel heavy now, but it is preparing you to stand under the weight of glory that is coming. And it will be good.

But we don't usually equate pain with goodness. Many of us are like me in that old British house. As soon as something goes wrong, we feel like God has abandoned us. Where is God when we're in pain? Is pain a result of God's absence? Is God present in pain? What is God's role in our suffering? How are we to understand God's presence and absence when we are going through physical turmoil? For answers to these questions, we will look at a book of the Bible called Job.

The Suffering of Job

Job contains one of the best treatments of suffering and the presence of God. Job was both a righteous and a wealthy man. He was so righteous, in fact, that his unwavering allegiance to God incited a debate between Satan and the Lord. Satan's thesis was that Job only remained a righteous man because God gave him every good thing. God hedged him in protection.

Good deeds in the midst of good things is nothing to be praised—or so Satan thought. So the Devil proposed a deal to test his thesis: "Stretch out your hand and strike everything he has, and he will surely curse you to your face" (Job 1:11 NIV). Though God knew Satan's thesis was incorrect, God agreed to his proposal with one limitation, "On the man himself do not lay a finger" (v. 12 NIV).

In one day, Job lost everything. His thousands upon thousands of livestock, his farms and houses, and most devastatingly, his ten children, were all taken from him. Everything was burned, scattered, or killed. Despite losing nearly all he had, Job fell to his knees and said, "Naked I came from my mother's womb, and naked shall I return. The LORD gave, and the LORD has taken away; blessed be the name of the LORD" (v. 21). Job worshipped God in his suffering because Job knew God was present in it.

There's another story of a man who worshipped God in his suffering that you may be more familiar with than you realize. His name was Horatio Spafford, and he was a modern-day Job. Horatio was a well-known and very successful lawyer in Chicago in the 1860s. He was a great man of faith and a respected Christian in his community. As his career thrived, he invested heavily in the booming Chicago real estate scene. Things could not have been going better for Horatio, his wife, and his four children.

However, in 1871, the great Chicago fire roared through the

city and destroyed most of Horatio's investments. He was reduced to nearly nothing. Needing to get away from it all, the Spafford family decided that they would take a trip to Europe. Horatio was delayed with work, so he sent his family ahead by boat, promising to meet up with them soon. But on November 22, 1873, the boat carrying Horatio's wife and four children sunk, killing 226 people, including all the Spafford children.

Horatio's wife, who was spared, sent a telegram from England informing her husband of the tragedy. Immediately Horatio set sail for his wife. During his long journey across the Atlantic, Horatio came upon the spot where the boat had sunk and his children had died. Looking out at the water, during all his suffering and torment, Horatio wrote the words of this now-famous hymn:

> *When peace, like a river, attendeth my way,*
> *When sorrows like sea billows roll;*
> *Whatever my lot, Thou hast taught me to say,*
> *It is well, it is well with my soul.*[2]

Horatio, like Job, knew that God was present in suffering. Far from this fact making him bitter, it spurred him on to worship God. When we go through hard times, the only proper response is worship. This is not some form of escape or denial but an acknowledgment that God is good, God is present, and God is in control.

Sovereign over Suffering

Not only does Job worship God and bless his name, he also recognizes the origin of his suffering. The devastation that fell on him came from God. But how can this be? The text says that the

Sabeans were the ones who killed the oxen and the donkeys. It was the Chaldeans who struck down the camels. As for Job's children, it was a windstorm that blew down the house in which they were eating, killing them all.[3] Wasn't it a murderous mob of angry men and the random outbreak of a natural disaster that caused the suffering? No.

Job knew who was really in control of all things. Before any of the suffering began, Satan had to acquire permission from God to do any harm to Job at all. Even Satan is required to operate inside of God's sovereign plan. Satan's statement to God, "stretch out your hand," was no recommendation or temptation, but a request. God knew that everything that was about to happen would bring about his own glory and Job's betterment. So God permitted Satan to harm Job. Only God's will can move his hand and cause anything to happen.

Job had spent his life thanking God for all the good things he had provided, and when God decided to take the good things away, Job knew and blessed the hand that took it. Satan's thesis was proven false.

But the Devil was persistent. He was certain all humans really wanted was to save their own skin. So Satan returned to God and reworded his thesis and request. "'Stretch out your hand and touch his bone and his flesh, and he will curse you to your face.' And the Lord said to Satan, 'Behold, he is in your hand; only spare his life'" (2:5–6). The parameters were set by God, not Satan. God was in control; Satan sought permission.

This time, when afflictions fell upon Job, it was not the Sabeans or the wind that beset Job, but Satan. "So Satan went out from the presence of the Lord and struck Job with loathsome sores from the sole of his foot to the crown of his head" (v. 7).

At this point, Job's wife finally spoke up. It's worth noting that from the moment God permitted it, Satan had dominion over the lives of all of Job's family. But when the rest of his family died, his wife was left alive. Satan had far more sinister plans for her. Once he attacked Job's physical body with boils and sores, his wife turned from her faith and invited Job to do the same: "Do you still hold fast your integrity?" she asked. "Curse God and die" (v. 9).

Satan knew that it would be easier for Job to see his wife die while trusting God than live while cursing him. It was a sick twist of Satan's knife. And for us, sometimes suffering is not just about what we've lost, but about what we're left with that turns to rot.

However, when Job's wife came to him and told him to curse God and die, Job responded by saying, "You speak as one of the foolish women would speak. Shall we receive good from God, and shall we not receive evil?" (v. 10). Wait a second, Job! Are you saying we receive evil from God's hand? Even though we read that it was Satan who struck him, Job knew that both good and evil ultimately come from the hand of God. And the Bible affirms Job's deduction to be true: "In all this Job did not sin with his lips" (v. 10).

Present and Active

This is where our understanding of God gets a hard gut check. We often equate suffering with God's absence. When times are hard, God must be far off. When times are good, God must be close. We often believe that joy means God is there and anguish means he isn't. But Job understood that God is present and active in both.

Hear this well: God is not absent when you are suffering. He is present, because his is the hand that gives both comfort and distress. God may be absent in the way we most desire, but he is present in the way we most require. He is absent as the one who will wipe away every tear, but present as the one who guides us into his kingdom through many tribulations.

God cannot be seen as absent in suffering because he is the sovereign cause behind it. Neither good fortune nor suffering is a sign of God's presence or absence; he is present in both. Most people don't like this conclusion—that God is the ultimate cause of suffering. However, Scripture demands that we see God as the ultimate cause of everything, whether good or evil.

> The Lord brings death and makes alive;
>> he brings down to the grave and raises up.
>>> (1 Sam. 2:6 niv)

> I form the light and create darkness,
>> I bring prosperity and create disaster;
>> I, the Lord, do all these things.
>>> (Isa. 45:7 niv)

> Who has spoken and it came to pass,
>> unless the Lord has commanded it?
> Is it not from the mouth of the Most High
>> that good and bad come?
>>> (Lam. 3:37–38)

> All the inhabitants of the earth are accounted as nothing,
>> and [God] does according to his will.
>>> (Dan. 4:35)

> The lot is cast into the lap,
>> but its every decision is from the Lord.
>>> (Prov. 16:33)

We cannot separate God's presence from our suffering. I know that the most natural response in times of trouble is to ask, *Where is God?* But God is never absent in his general presence and sovereignty. You may be going through one of the hardest times in your life right now. The only certain part of your faith at the moment may be your assurance that God is absent.

I promise you, God is not absent. He has not resigned from caring for you. You have, no doubt, heard promises like this before, but I know that sometimes theology just doesn't help. People telling you more about God, what we may call theology, does not always give us the comfort we are looking for. However, I believe if we speak directly to the root cause of our distress—the perceived absence of God in our suffering—we will begin to talk about some theology that is quite helpful.

Innocent Suffering

Suffering is not just hard because of the affliction it causes; it's harder still because of the questions it raises. Perhaps Job was one of the first people to ask, *Why is God doing this to me?* Job rightly understood that he was a righteous and upstanding man, and God continually affirmed this. However, Job believed God was punishing him in spite of his righteousness. Job's logic may have gone something like this:

1. I am righteous and do not deserve to suffer.
2. God is making me suffer regardless of my righteousness.
3. Therefore, is God unjust for making me suffer?

Is there such a thing as innocent suffering? The book of Job argues that, in a sense, there is. We could perhaps more accurately call this type of suffering "non-retributive suffering"—suffering that is not a result of direct retribution. God wasn't punishing Job because of a specific sin, so in that view he was "innocent." This was non-retributive suffering.

Many of us have heard from some well-intentioned friend, "Don't you know that no one is innocent?" In fact, the miserable companions Job was forced into conversation with say pretty much the same thing: "Can a mortal be more righteous than God? Can even a strong man be more pure than his Maker?" (Job 4:17 NIV).

Job never questioned whether he was perfect or equal with God. He did, however, question God's justice and fairness. Did his few sins merit the extreme catastrophes that had overtaken him? No. The same could be said of an abuse victim. Does the young student who spends her time studying, socializing with friends, and going to church deserve to be harmed in such a manner? Of course not.

So then, innocent—or rather, non-retributive—suffering does exist. We're sinners, sure, but our sin and suffering isn't always on a one-for-one scale.[4] If that were true, many corrupt powerful people would be impoverished and powerless, and many godly impoverished people would be well off. God doesn't dole out blessings and punishments on a strict retribution scale. In fact, the opposite is often true. Not all suffering is an equal response to an equal offense.

But God has a plan in all our suffering that is far better than any life without it. Did you catch that? Since God is the Author of all things, the life and the world in which we live—with all its suffering—is far better, for our good and his glory, than any universe that could ever have existed without all this pain. God uses suffering and trials to make us holier. This is a process called sanctification.

There's a good chance you're going through something difficult right now; maybe it's even the worst season of your life. Please hear me: God loves you, and he is present in your pain. It's far less likely that you are being punished because of a sin (retribution) and far more likely that you are being put through a trial in order to kill sin (sanctification). I'm sure you have many more questions right now, but please do not let one of them be, *What have I done to deserve this?*

Putting God on Trial

When we ask, *What have I done to deserve this?* we are essentially putting God on trial. That was Job's big mistake. In doing this, we are bringing God's justice and judgment into question. Out of all the people who have ever asked this question, perhaps none may be seen as more worthy to ask it than Elie Wiesel.

Wiesel was a prisoner at the Nazi concentration camp Auschwitz. He endured and observed the extremes of horror that one person can suffer at the hands of another. From starvation to mass extermination to the hanging of children, Elie Wiesel saw so much horror that he put God on trial.

Wiesel barely survived the terrors of the concentration camp. Upon his return home, he wrote about what he had endured. One scene retells the vicious hanging of two men and a child.

> Then came the march past the victims. The two men were no longer alive. Their tongues were hanging out, swollen and bluish. But the third rope was still moving: the child, too light, was still breathing . . . And so he remained for more than half an hour, lingering between life and death, writhing before our eyes.

And we were forced to look at him at close range. He was still alive when I passed him. His tongue was still red, his eyes not yet extinguished. Behind me, I heard the same man asking: "For God's sake, where is God?" And from within me, I heard a voice answer: "Where is He? This is where—hanging here from this gallows."[5]

The experience of suffering killed Wiesel's God. If God would allow this, Wiesel thought, then he must not exist. No God that would allow this much suffering could possibly be real. Wiesel put God on trial and found him guilty of absence, injustice, and nonexistence. What Wiesel didn't realize was that the existence of suffering doesn't disprove the existence of God. The presence of pain does not prove the absence of God. This misunderstanding stems from a belief that humans don't deserve to suffer and a good God would never allow it.

Job mounted his own case against God but came to a very different conclusion. He realized that God was not in the seat of the accused but the judge with the final say. Job confessed, "How then can I dispute with him? How can I find words to argue with him? Though I were innocent, I could not answer him; I could only plead with my Judge for mercy" (9:14–15 NIV).

Job recognized the fine line between innocent suffering and non-retributive suffering. We've already established that Job did not deserve all the pain he was going through on a perfect this-sin-for-that-punishment scale. But now Job was pointing out that no one is truly innocent, for all have sinned against God. In acknowledging his own sin and God's perfection, Job saw the problem in asking, *Why do bad things happen to good people?* because there are no truly good people. In the full light of God, none of us are truly innocent. We are all sin-stained people, worthy of suffering.

We are not entitled to a carefree or pain-free life—though it is what many of us believe we deserve. A perfect existence, free from suffering, is no one's right. You and I have harmed many people, either consciously or unconsciously, through our actions. Why, then, do we believe we should be free from the pain brought upon us by anyone or anything else?

Yet, despite our sin, we tend to believe that we are (somehow) the exception to the rule. That was Job's problem. The hardest pill for Job to swallow was his own integrity. He could not find enough fault within himself to merit such suffering from the hand of God. So Job's questions continued:

> *Does it please you to oppress me,*
> *to spurn the work of your hands,*
> *while you smile on the plans of the wicked? . . .*
> *Are your days like those of a mortal*
> *or your years like those of a strong man,*
> *that you must search out my faults*
> *and probe after my sin—*
> *though you know that I am not guilty*
> *and that no one can rescue me from your hand?*
>
> (10:3, 5–7 NIV)

Job was essentially saying, "Why are you picking on me? Does causing me such grief make you happy? Are you some kind of sadist?"

Like Job, many of us have experienced suffering and demanded answers. We've put God on the witness stand. We cannot see what we have done to deserve the suffering we are going through, and we can't imagine any defense from God that could explain his actions. In our cross-examination of the Almighty, we can end up painting God as a kid on an anthill burning us with his extra-large magnifying glass, laughing at the spectacle of our squirming. If we cannot separate God from suffering by saying he is absent in it, then he must be present with some cruel intent.

Let's be clear: God is *not* present in suffering because he enjoys tormenting us. He is present in suffering because he loves us. A disinterested god would have turned his back on Job while Satan did his bidding. Our loving God puts limits on suffering and brings good out of it. A vengeful God would have smote Job at the first questioning of his justice. Our gracious God allowed Job to vent his frustrations before responding.

When you really drill down into it, removing God from suffering provides no comfort at all. Would you really rather the world and all its suffering be the product of mankind's evil, running out of control? Would you rather blame happenstance and randomness for evil, waiting to see who it will take next? Would you rather place all the blame on Satan, a powerful spirit let off the leash? Or would you rather, in times of trouble, be able to look at the worst situation and say, "This is horrific, but I know God is near"?

It is far better to live in a world with a present God and great suffering than to live in a world with an absent God and no suffering. We would have far more to fear in our suffering if it were all a matter of Satan or circumstance. I would much rather suffer at the hands of my loving Father than at the murderous hands of the Devil or the cruel hands of fate. I would much prefer to writhe under the agony of a corrective rod than under the malicious striking of Satan or the random hammer of happenstance. I would take the loving punishment of a kind God over the hateful torment of a fallen angel or the unexplainable pain of random occurrence. I would take the guiding crook of the Shepherd over the sadistic whim of demons or the aimless stream of chance.

I would take the presence of God in my suffering anytime.

You Are Not God

When I was very young, I stole an eraser from a local Christian bookstore in my city. It had a cartoon picture of Noah's ark on it, and for some reason I had to have it. After asking my mom to buy it for me and being denied, I did something I had never done before: I stole. Upon arriving home, I got my new eraser out and began to look at it with delight and shame. During my infatuated inspection, my mother crept up beside me and asked, "Where did you get that?"

She knew the answer already. I was hauled off to my dad, who drove me back to the bookstore and made me return the eraser to the store's manager. And I didn't just have to return it. My dad insisted on the manager telling me why stealing from the store hurt him, his employees, and the people who made the eraser. I learned my lesson.

But imagine if I'd refused to return the eraser to the manager. After my dad had driven me to the store and dragged me inside, what if I had stopped in the middle of the shop and started assaulting my dad with questions: "Why are you doing this to me? Why is stealing wrong? Why can't I keep the eraser I took?" People passing by would probably laugh. Why? Because a child has no authority over a parent.

The act of questioning may be permitted, but the parent is under no obligation to answer. A parent is not subject to the child but the other way around. It's humbling for us to think of ourselves as children, but when Jesus taught us to pray, the prayer began, "Our Father in heaven" (Matt. 6:9). To confess his fatherhood is to admit our childhood. And after all of Job's questioning, he was about to be reminded who was in charge.

At the end of the book, God himself showed up and revealed a mighty manifestation of his presence to Job.[6] Not only was God never absent in Job's suffering, he was now no longer absent to Job's eyes and ears. Job knocked on God's door with his massive list of questions. In response, God knocked down Job's door with an even greater list of riddles. Much like Moses asking to see God's glory, Job asked for more of God and got more than he asked for.

When God showed up, he didn't defend himself, but he did demand a defense from Job. The Lord said to Job, "Brace yourself like a man; I will question you, and you shall answer me. Where were you when I laid the earth's foundation? Tell me, if you understand. Who marked off its dimensions? Surely you know! Who stretched a measuring line across it?" (38:3–5 NIV).

God continued presenting Job with unanswerable questions about where the vaults of hailstones are kept, where light is stored, and how to cut a path for a rainstorm. Job was altogether unable to answer these questions. So he bleakly eked out, "I am unworthy— how can I reply to you? I put my hand over my mouth. I spoke once, but I have no answer—twice, but I will say no more" (40:4–5 NIV).

The point of God's bombardment of question after question was to show how foolish Job's ranting was. Job was the child who stole an eraser and then self-righteously questioned his parent as to why it was wrong. It was not as if God could not have given answers to Job's questions. But rather, Job's questions were so meager compared to the hidden things of God. The greatest mystery in the world is not why people suffer, but how God goes about being God. Wells of ink have been spilled addressing the problem of pain.[7] But not one serious author would dare to lay one stroke of the pen to one leaf of paper in any attempt to answer even one of the questions God poses to Job. The hidden wisdom of God is beyond our understanding.

But God's wisdom will not be fully hidden forever. One day we will know the purpose of our sufferings; we will see the fruit of our affliction. First Corinthians 13:8–10 tells us, "Where there are prophecies, they will cease; where there are tongues, they will be stilled; where there is knowledge, it will pass away. For we know in part and we prophesy in part, but when completeness comes, what is in part disappears" (NIV). Just as we long for the immediate, actual presence of God, we also deeply desire the knowledge we will have when we are with him.

In the same way I desired to be in God's actual presence while singing "I Can Only Imagine" in my Red 2 classroom, I also long to see the world through the eyes and knowledge of God, especially in the midst of my sufferings. But those black trash bags of absence cloud our vision. Just as God cannot be experienced perfectly or immediately in this life, neither can knowledge be had perfectly or immediately. Some things will remain unknown to us until that day.

However, we can go forward in our sufferings with the knowledge that God is present in them. That is why James could say, "Consider it pure joy, my brothers and sisters, whenever you face trials of many kinds, because you know that the testing of your faith produces perseverance" (1:2–3 NIV).

Suffering can be considered a joy when we know that our good God is present in it. We have no ground on which to call God to the witness stand and judge him for causing us to suffer. We are far too guilty and far too finite to bring any charge against him or understand his reasons. We will always be the kid with the stolen eraser in our hands and ludicrous questions on our lips. In faith, we are to consider our sufferings joy. Not blindly or in ignorance, but in a sure knowledge that though God is absent in the way we most desire, he is surely present in the way we most require—even if that presence brings pain.

The Weight of Glory

Suffering in absence prepares us for presence. Second Corinthians 4:17 gives us a glimpse at the eternal plan God has for our suffering:

"This light momentary affliction is preparing for us an eternal weight of glory beyond all comparison." There is a weight to glory that we must be prepared for. Our feet must learn to walk across the sharp grass of heaven so that we may run in the fields of grace. Our skin must learn to withstand the storm clouds of suffering so that we may dance in the rain of salvation. Pain prepares us for presence.

We are not only called to prepare for the weight of glory but to wait for glory. The glory we wait for is the reception of our new, perfect, heavenly bodies. Our glorification—the remaking of our earthly bodies into new eternal bodies—will occur when we are made able to stand before the glory of God.

We are not only called to prepare ourselves to stand before the glory of God but to await our own glorification by the hand of God. There will come a day when those who believe in Christ will be glorified. All pain will become a memory, suffering will be an artifact of history, and death will be forgotten inside never-ending life. We will stand before our Father in heaven and hear the words, "Well done, good and faithful servant" (Matt. 25:21).

We are built to give God glory, yet God prepares a way to give us glory. The glory God bestows upon us is his approval. We will become admired by the most admirable being. We will become glorified by the only one who may be called glorious. As C. S. Lewis said, in his sermon entitled "The Weight of Glory," "The redeemed soul, beyond all hope and nearly beyond belief, learns at last that she has pleased Him whom she was created to please."[8] The weight is worth the wait. Pain prepares us for presence. Suffering paves the road to glory.

Nowhere is this truer than in the cross of Christ. The suffering of Jesus paved our road to glory. The pain of Jesus earned for us the pleasure of presence. For as often as we want to put God on trial in our suffering, God could far more often and with far surpassing reason put us on trial. We are guilty of breaking his eternal law, desecrating his image held in our bodies, and staining his good world with our transgressions.

We deserve to be on trial, not God. Yet, though we deserve to be prosecuted to the extremes of the law, God does not put us on trial. Instead, he put himself on trial. He suffered as the God-man, Jesus. He bore more pain than could possibly befall us in this life. He took on far more suffering than we blame him for. We aren't rejected by God in our pain. Jesus was rejected by God in his pain.

We do not need to blame God for our pain or believe that he is absent in it, for he took our blame and our pain when he became present to us in the person of Jesus Christ.

TEN

THAT SAFE DARKNESS

Where is God in the darkness?

*You have wrapped yourself with a cloud
so that no prayer can pass through.*
—LAMENTATIONS 3:44

call, I cling, I want—and there is no One to answer. . . . Where
I try to raise my thoughts to Heaven—there is such convicting
emptiness that those very thoughts return like sharp knives &
hurt my very soul.—Love—the word—it brings nothing.—I am
told God loves me—and yet the reality of darkness & coldness &
emptiness is so great that nothing touches my soul."[1]

These are the words of Mother Teresa.

Mother Teresa, originally named Gonxha Agnes Bojaxhiu, was
born in 1910 and raised in a pious Catholic home in Macedonia.
At eighteen, she joined the Sisters of Loreto and was given the

name Sister Mary Teresa. The Dublin-based order of Loreto ran missions in India, and that is where Teresa was sent.

While on a train from Calcutta to Darjeeling, Mother Teresa said she heard the voice of Jesus telling her to leave her own religious order for the sake of serving the poor. So she moved to Calcutta. She helped the poor and the sick and was known for helping the terminally ill die with dignity, joy, and comfort.

But it was not just good deeds that drew the world's attention to the poor Catholic nun—a nun serving the poor doesn't usually make headlines. Mother Teresa garnered a special audience because of her way with words. She has been called the "poet laureate of the soul" and the "sound-bite saint." Her writings have encouraged millions into a more radical service of Jesus.

So it was no surprise that some of her letters were released following her death in 1997. However, the world was shocked to discover the extreme struggle with doubt her letters revealed. For nearly fifty years, from 1948 till her death, Mother Teresa wrote privately as one in spiritual anguish, with only one month of relief in 1958.

Listen to a few of her other laments: "I did not know that love could make one suffer so much . . . of pain human but caused by divine."[2] "The more I want Him—the less I am wanted.—I want to love Him as He has not been loved—and yet there is that separation—that terrible emptiness, that feeling of absence of God."[3]

Mother Teresa experienced the same desire as Moses—more wanted more. She was so in love with God that the absence of his actual and immediate presence was insufferable to her. A distance lay between her and God that some may see as closeness. But to a lover, even an inch of distance can seem like an infinite gap. An inch can feel like absence. The more Mother Teresa loved God, the farther she felt from him.

Hearing God's Call

There is a great story of what it feels like to be far from God in the life of the prophet Jonah. As she told it, Mother Teresa was on a train when God spoke to her, but Scripture does not reveal what Jonah was doing when God came and audibly spoke to him.[4] We can assume he was going about his normal life. However, this presence of God was far from normal. God revealed the presence of his voice to Jonah.

The prophet was chosen by God to take a message of repentance to the people of Nineveh, who were known for their violence and wickedness. Though a mighty call was now on his life, Jonah was fearful for his own safety and bitter that God would be willing to save such a wicked people. Nineveh, after all, was a horribly violent town—nicknamed "the city of blood."[5] Jonah wanted nothing to do with this call.

So Jonah did his best to flee from God. He quickly made his way to the sea, where he hired a boat bound in the opposite direction of God's call. Jonah was now bound for a port city called Tarshish. He thought that putting distance between himself and the location where God showed up would put distance between his responsibility and the command of the Lord. Jonah was not only trying to escape the presence of God. He was trying to flee from the will of God.

The presence and will of God are inescapable. This was Jonah's first lesson regarding the presence and absence of God: we don't get to decide when God is absent and when he is present. Only God can do that. When Jonah tried to run away from the location of God's presence, he found his escape attempt as futile as trying to outrun the air. You may think that you have put too much distance between yourself and God over the years, but that is impossible. There is nowhere you can flee where God is not already present.[6]

Neither the presence nor the command of God can be escaped by any swiftness of the legs, any distance of the sea, or in any depth of the earth. When God sets his choice upon an individual, his chase is fiercer than any gale. Like a seasoned hunting dog after its prey, when the scent of our souls is placed in his nostrils, no escape can prove successful.

Francis Thompson, author of the famous poem "The Hound of Heaven," captured God's chase of us with visceral imagery:

> *I fled Him, down the nights and down the days;*
> *I fled Him, down the arches of the years;*
> *I fled Him, down the labyrinthine ways*
> *Of my own mind; and in the mist of tears*
> *I hid from Him, and under running laughter.*
> *Up vistaed hopes I sped;*
> *And shot, precipitated,*
> *Adown Titanic glooms of chasmed fears,*
> *From those strong Feet that followed, followed after.*
> *But with unhurrying chase,*
> *And unperturbed pace,*
> *Deliberate speed, majestic instancy,*
> *They beat—and a Voice beat*
> *More instant than the Feet—*
> *"All things betray thee, who betrayest Me."*[7]

No matter how long it has been since you've pulled into the church parking lot. No matter how many times you've turned your back on Jesus. No matter how often you drop your cross to pick up old habits. No matter how far gone you think you are from God's will. No matter how dark the night of your soul may be. You cannot run from heaven's hound.

Your flight from God and his demand on your life is just as vain as Jonah's flight to the ships sailing far from Nineveh. All your Christian life you may have thought it was you who was pursuing God, but all along it has been God pursuing you. So no matter how long it has been since you have looked toward the Father, no matter how absent you believe God is, neither the steps of your feet nor the sin of your life can move you one inch away from God's love if you are in Christ Jesus. It may feel like absence now, but presence is hot on your trail—even though it may come upon you like a storm.

The Last Resort

As Jonah sailed away from where he thought God was, the Lord sent a great storm upon the sea that threatened to capsize Jonah's boat along with all the men onboard. The sailors threw their cargo overboard to lighten the ship's load, but she was still going under. Finally, Jonah understood that the storm was the hand of God. The fleeing prophet told the sailors to throw him overboard, promising that the sea would calm as soon as they did. He knew God had come for him and him alone.[8]

Don't forget: when Jonah told the sailors to throw him overboard, he knew nothing of the fish that was soon to come and swallow him up. Jonah was resigning himself to death. He was requesting the crew's help for his assisted suicide. Jonah realized that fleeing his home and responsibilities could not separate him from God or the call God had placed on his life. But there was one last resort: death. Jonah sought out death as a means of complete absence from God and his call.

Let me be clear: I'm not saying Jonah was trying to die as a way of spiting God. Jonah first fled in fear and disobedience. He asked to be flung to his death out of guilt and defeat.

"Pick me up and throw me into the sea," Jonah said, "and it will become calm. I know that it is my fault that this great storm has come upon you" (1:12 NIV). This was Jonah's mea culpa. In Jonah's mind, there was no going back; there was no repentance; there was no accepting the call of God now. He had wandered too far. He judged death to be the only relief from the guilt he was feeling. God was too angry to accept him now. The hound had bared his teeth.

If we are honest, most of us would admit there's been a time in our lives when we felt like abandoning our faith altogether. "I've wandered this far, I might as well finish the job. I should just stop believing." "I'm not worthy of this faith anyway." "I'm far too sinful to be saved now." Jumping ship seems to be the only possible punctuation mark to put on the end of the sentence our lives have written. When those storms come, it's easy to think the only way things will calm down is if we just give up. Perhaps this is the state your faith is in—somewhere between the place where God originally called out to you and the bottom of the ocean floor.

Encountering the inescapable presence of God as a guilty sinner can cause us to consider terrible things, for our guilt is terrible. But no amount of running, self-harm, or even death can separate you from God, your guilt, or the command he has placed on your life. Whether in this life or the next, God will swallow you up in his provision and deal with you as he wishes. For Jonah, the swallowing was done by a large fish.

The Belly

Jonah jumped overboard into the murderous sea. The water closed around his nose and mouth. But before he could drown, "the LORD appointed a great fish to swallow up Jonah" (1:17).

God often arranges our circumstances to be what is needed for us to best experience his presence—even if that experience feels like absence or darkness. It was the provision and presence of God that put Jonah into the dark belly of the fish. God saved Jonah's life by placing him in darkness.

Jonah found God at the end of his rope. Jonah left all hope behind and gave his body up to the swallowing mouth of the sea. But before God would allow Jonah to destroy himself, the Lord provided a rescue for him. Jonah thought he was in his darkest hour, but God rescued him by taking him even farther into the darkness of a fish's belly. Jonah thought he was at his lowest point, but God took him lower within the body of a beast.

When we are at our lowest, God may bring us lower still. When we are at our darkest point, God may take us to even darker places for our good. No matter how dark things seem, God is present. No matter how far you've run, God is not tired. God may feel absent or angry to you, but even after you've thrown yourself away, God can still swallow you up in the safe darkness of his provision and presence.

For Jonah, the belly of the fish may have been a physical representation of the "dark night of the soul." The phrase "dark night of the soul" comes from the title of a sixteenth-century Spanish poem. The poem details what happens to a soul when it finds itself in the valley of absence. When the soul is blind to the presence of God, it is said to be in the dark night.

The poem speaks of God as very near even when darkness is present. This is seen most clearly in the line, "With his gentle hand he wounded my neck and caused all my senses to be suspended. I remained, lost in oblivion."[9] When God's hand comes near, it can feel like a wounding.

St. John of the Cross, the poem's author, was saying that a

soul is thrown into darkness when God comes closer than we can handle. It's counterintuitive, but nearness can be the cause of distance. God may feel far, but that may mean that he is actually quite near. If God feels far from you, it may be because he has drawn so near to you that you have been put into darkness. The light of God's closeness can cause the darkness of his absence.

Light That Causes Darkness

How can light cause darkness? Think of it this way: When you are first waking up in the morning, your eyes have been closed for several hours. All the lights are out, and you peek through one eye to turn on the screen of your phone. The light of the phone's screen, which we stare at for hours during the day, is now like looking straight at the sun. It blinds us, gives us a headache, and makes us squint or close our eyes altogether. Light can be so bright that it causes darkness, even blindness.

I remember being in elementary school and making a cardboard apparatus out of a shoebox and a toilet paper roll in order to look at the sun without hurting my eyes. I recall how confused I was by the fact that we can look at the world that is illuminated by the sun all day, but we cannot look at the sun itself without harming our eyes. The same is true about different types of God's presence. His general presence illuminates all that we see in the world. However, the relational presence of his drawing near can be much more like looking straight at the sun. There is a brightness that causes darkness.

We have been looking at God through cardboard tubes, and now he has come near. We are staring at the sun and are cast into darkness. St. John of the Cross put it this way: "The clearer and more manifest are Divine things in themselves the darker and more hidden are they to the soul naturally."[10] The eyes of our soul are not attuned to the brightness of God. We cannot make sense of God's presence, so we are thrown into confusion. We cannot see clearly what this dazzling light is, so we interpret it as darkness. All we see around us is the blackness of the fish's belly, when in fact we are nestled inside the providence and presence of God.

For presence is exactly what the darkness of the fish's belly was. God brought the dark night of the belly to spare Jonah's life. It must have been a horrendous existence, living in that fish. But God had plans for Jonah's life and chose to save it any way he could. The fish was God's provision and presence, though to Jonah its insides were pitch-black. Sometimes when God draws close to provide for us, it throws us into darkness.

The light not only blinds us, it also torments us in a way. Listen to the words of David the psalmist: "Look away from me, that I may smile again, before I depart and am no more!"[11] When the soul encounters the direct attention of God, the pain that results can be immense. The pure light of God reveals our impurities. I love the words of J. C. Ryle on this subject: "The nearer [a Christian] draws to God, and the more he sees of God's holiness and perfection, the more thoroughly is he sensible of his own countless imperfections."[12]

This stark contrast causes us to believe that God is against us. When the light of God's presence draws near, we are filled with a tormenting sense that God is so opposed to us that we could never find favor with him. We believe God has rejected us.

It's like a middle-school kid practicing his jump shot at a gym. He feels pretty confident about his shot until an NBA player comes in and starts sinking every three-pointer he puts up. The comparison throws him into darkness. Or think of it like trying to hang up a large picture frame. I'm one of those people who tries to level the things they hang on the wall by eyeballing it. But as soon as I get something hung up on the wall, my wife comes by with a level and reveals just how terribly off my attempt was. It wasn't until the standard came that I felt bad about my work.

When the perfect God comes close to us, we are struck with just how imperfect we are. The closer we get to God, the farther he can feel because the level is placed squarely on our lives. God can draw so close that we are blinded by the comparison.

This is exactly what Mother Teresa was going through when she penned the words that opened this chapter. She wrote elsewhere, "They say people in hell suffer eternal pain because of the loss of God . . . In my soul I feel just this terrible pain of loss, of God not wanting me, of God not being God, of God not really existing. . . . Heaven from every side is closed."[13]

It is a terrible thing to feel like God is absent. It is another pain altogether to feel like he is present but has rejected you. To be so wrapped up in the belly of the fish that you forget who it was that put you there. To be so oppressed by the darkness around you that you forget the providence that saved your life. If you think you may be in darkness now because of the light, I want to encourage you with a simple fact: your eyes will adjust.

The longer we look into the light, the more clearly we will begin to see everything else, much like when we look at our phone in the middle of the night. It blinds us for the first few seconds, but eventually we can see clearly. We pick up our phone, even though we know it will sting our eyes, because we want to look at that which it illuminates. God's light will show itself to be beautiful and will illuminate everything else around it as well. Keep looking into the light no matter how dark your darkness gets. Your eyes will adjust.

That Safe Darkness

The darkness may not be comfortable, but it is safe. It is safe for two reasons. First, the darkness is the presence and provision of God. Without the fish, Jonah would have died at sea. The darkness of our souls may be the very means by which God rescues us. It may be the means by which he makes us walk in his ways (see Ezek. 36:27). The darkness is safe because it keeps us from leaning upon ourselves. It pulls us out of the waves and into the belly, the very place God prepared for us to be.

Second, the darkness is safe because it moves us toward God and his plan, even if we are unaware of it. Tarshish was in the opposite direction of Nineveh. Not only was Jonah running away from God, he was running in the exact opposite direction from the place to which God had called him. Nineveh was a six-hundred-mile trek across land. However, Tarshish was a twenty-three-hundred-mile journey across the sea. Jonah was willing to travel twenty-nine-hundred miles in the opposite direction to escape God and his call.

We don't know how far into his journey Jonah was before God had him thrown overboard. But what I love about this story is that while Jonah was in the blackness of the belly, God was taking Jonah where he wanted the prophet to go. God brings us to himself in the safe darkness. As Gerald May, a psychiatrist exploring the connection between darkness and spiritual growth, put it, "Sometimes the only way we can enter the deeper dimensions of the journey is by being unable to see where we're going."[14]

It would be like a woman waking up to her home being completely engulfed in flames. She is still in bed and is incapacitated by fear. Firefighters charge into her room, but she clings to her bed and begins kicking the rescuers out of confusion and terror. In order to save her life, the firefighters gently and professionally knock her out so that they can carry her to safety. Sometimes the only way to be rescued is if we don't know it's happening.

God blinds us to move us. He puts us in darkness in order to lead us to places we would have never gone on our own. We are made to do what we do not want to do despite our apprehensions and fear. The dark night blinds us so that God can carry us away from our own intentions. God moves us along his path in the safe darkness.

You may feel like you are at a standstill. You may think you are moving farther away from God. You may even think that God is not in the darkness at all. But God is moving you to himself, even when you are in the belly of blackness.

Regurgitation and Resurrection

Jonah was a foreshadowing of Jesus. In Matthew 12:38–40, some of the religious leaders of the day approached Jesus and requested a sign. They wanted Jesus to prove, through some kind of miracle, that he had been sent from God. Jesus responded, "An evil and adulterous generation seeks for a sign, but no sign will be given to it except the sign of the prophet Jonah. For just as Jonah was three days and three nights in the belly of the great fish, so will the Son of Man be three days and three nights in the heart of the earth."

The three nights Jonah spent in the fish's belly were a foretelling of the three nights Jesus would spend in the tomb. Likewise, the regurgitation of Jonah by the fish is the forerunner of the resurrection of Jesus from the tomb. The sign of Jonah is the resurrection of Jesus from the grave.

In the belly of the great fish, Jonah did not know that he would ever see the light of day again—for he had done nothing to deserve a second chance. However, God was faithful to Jonah and commanded his release from darkness. How sudden that propulsion from the belly of blackness must have been for Jonah. How involuntarily and unexpectedly his freedom into the light must have come.

But we are not like Jonah. We have a sure knowledge that we will escape the dark night of the soul. In this life or the next, whether upon the shores of this world or the banks of heaven, the belly of blackness will release us from its grip. I will not give you false hope. Mother Teresa died before the dark night of her soul ever lifted. She was tormented by the divine Light until she left this earth to dwell in it.

The hope we must cling to through the dark nights of our souls must not be to escape the belly itself. It must be to remain in the divine Light no matter if it is torturous and no matter if it takes us to our death. We cling to Christ and his resurrection.

We know we will escape the darkness of absence, not because of any good we have done or because God feels close, but because we have been given the sign of Jonah. We will break out of the darkness because Christ is risen from the grave.

Our spiritual assurance in this life does not come from how we feel. Our confidence in our own salvation is not tied to how close or far God appears to be. The only reason we can be sure that we will break out of absence's blackness when we die and enter the light of God's presence is because Jesus broke the blackness of the grave and now sits at the right hand of God. The sign of Jonah is our hope in the belly. The resurrection of Jesus is our light in the darkness.

We often believe that whatever we feel is true. Therefore, if we feel condemned, separated, unworthy, and without hope, surely that must be the state of our souls. John Piper talked about this time in the Christian's life in his short book on waiting for God called *When the Darkness Will Not Lift*. Piper wrote, "The darkest experience for the child of God is when his faith sinks out of his own sight. Not out of God's sight, but his. Yes, it is possible to be so overwhelmed with darkness that you do not know if you are a Christian—and yet still be one."[15]

There are times when our own salvation slips from our sight. But it never slips from the sight of God.[16] You may not be confident in the state of your soul, but God always is. Though our confidence may waiver, his presence never does.

This is where the good news of the sign of Jonah comes in: salvation is not based on our assurance but on Christ's resurrection. We may be in the belly of the great fish, but God is leading us to the shores of salvation. We may not know which way we are going, but God is moving us within that safe darkness. Our own salvation may be far from our sight, but if God saved us from the waves while we swam in the daylight, he is sure to rescue us while we sit in the dark night of the soul.

THE GOSPEL OF NEARNESS

Absence Makes Sense

Absence is
The only response
That makes sense if
We take into account
God's holiness and justice
Along with the astounding amount
Of our sinfulness.

Absence is
The only response
That makes sense.

And this absence
Could have happened
Through one of two actions
With the same consequence.

God, in his holiness, could have abandoned us
Or, in his justice, could have destroyed us—
And either would have ended our existence.

That would have made more sense.
That would have been more obvious.
If God, being the very definition of goodness,
The very creator of righting injustices,
Had removed himself from the world
Or simply done away with it.

But God's presence with creation was not finished.

Yes, God did withdraw
But he offered a promise.

He gave us a hope
Without refusing to punish.

He told us he would return
But did not refuse to leave us.

God removed us from himself
But still pointed us to Jesus.

He wrote the conclusion in the preface.
He put the climax in the leaflet.
God put the end of Revelation
At the very beginning of Genesis.

Because though the serpent

Led Adam and Eve to make themselves dead,
The same God who removed them from the garden
Would return to crush that demon's head.

That is the part that doesn't make sense:
He who had every right to be absent
Would make himself present.

He who had every justification
To remove his glory from our midst
Would remove himself from his glory
To take on our sins.

He who created men
Who then created absence
Became like one of them
To remove that distance.

Absence may be
The only
Response that makes sense,

But presence is
The only conclusion
That can exist
Once we understand
That the God who isn't there
Is the God who came near
In the person and the love of Jesus.

ELEVEN

GOD WITH US

How should I understand

the presence of Jesus?

"Whoever has seen me has seen the Father.
How can you say, 'Show us the Father'?"
—JOHN 14:9

Scary things are not for me. I cannot sit through a scary movie. I refuse to go into a haunted house. I don't even like walking around my house late at night when all the lights are out. I don't know what it is; I'm just not too fond of things that go bump in the night. There was one night in my childhood I will never forget because of how filled with terror it was.

When I was still in elementary school, my family and I moved houses. We weren't traveling far from my childhood home, but we still had to pack up the house. One of the most difficult things to prepare for the move was my parents' bed. In fact, it was going to be so hard to move that they decided to deconstruct it so they could give it away.

This seemed like a travesty to me because it was no ordinary mattress and spring bed; it was a king-size waterbed. While all the other kids on my block had to settle for jumping on their parents' bed, I got to go surfing, swimming, wriggling, and rolling around on that surface of plastic water. I loved that bed, and now I had to watch it go.

If that wasn't torturous enough, my dad had a task for me that would prove to be the last straw for my sanity. In order to break down the bed, the massive amounts of water had to be drained first. So my dad hooked up a hose to the bed's valve, snaked it through hallways and out the door into the street. My job was to sit on the curb, next to the hose, and alert my dad when the water started flowing freely out. This wouldn't have been bad at all, but night had already fallen.

As I followed the coiling hose through the house, I came to the screen door and stopped. Peering out into my dark street, I couldn't even make out where the green garden tube ended. It was a black land of unknown horrors. But wanting to be a good son and prove to my dad that I could handle the task, I took a deep breath and followed the green line out into the abyss.

Standing on the edge of our lawn, I fixed my eyes on the threaded brass tip of the hose. I waited for what seemed like an eternity for a drop to trickle out. The world began to change around me. The once-familiar sound of cars whizzing by on distant streets morphed into the encroaching broomsticks of flying evil witches about to descend on my position. The shadows cast by passing headlights turned the branches of trees into quick moving hands, reaching out to drag me to my doom. I was freaking out. I wanted water to come out of that hose more than anything in all of existence. I waited.

Finally, a weak trickle spilled out of the brass tip, then stopped.

Water had come, but not the water I was waiting for. I needed a steady flow to start coming out before I could report back to my dad. The shadows grew more aggressive, the whooshing brooms overhead fluttered with more madness. Every minute or so another weak squirt would pitifully fall out of the hose's mouth. Each time my anticipation and anxiety grew.

At length, the sound of water could be heard running up the snake's belly. My expectation soared. Soon water was flowing freely as the bed I so loved finally began draining itself for the last time. I bolted across the lawn, keeping my steps wide and my knees high, because I was certain that if I didn't, some undead hand would shoot up from the dirt and snag my ankles. I made it to the porch and flew open the screen door. I ran to my dad and jumped into his arms with tears in my eyes. "The water is flowing," I said. My dad hugged me, told me everything was going to be all right and that I was safe.

Ever since the fall of Adam and Eve, the people of Israel had been standing out on the front lawn of the world waiting for the water to start flowing. They had been told that God was coming. Israel was instructed to wait for the coming Messiah, the Holy One sent from God. This Messiah would set them free, deliver them from sin, and bring presence into their absence. God would be with man.

However, for most of Israel's history, all they could see were little spurts from the hose of God's promise and the darkness closing in. Where was this fountain of living water? When would it start to flow freely? How long would they have to put up with little trickles while the world closed in on them? Where was God?

God would be silent for hundreds of years. Then one small stream of his words would come out of a prophet. God would feel absent for multiple generations. Then one person would have an encounter with this elusive God. And the darkness around them was not a fantasy or a product of fear. There were no imagined witches or shadowing tree hands. They had been in slavery and exiled, had been occupied and forced into labor. God had promised them that he would be with them as their king, but he was nowhere to be found. The coming Messiah was absent.

That was, until Jesus entered the world and turned the spigot on full blast. Finally the anticipated water was flowing into the streets. The long-hoped-for Messiah showed up, right where God had promised. Water was no longer absent from the brass mouth of the Bible's story. Glory was gushing out of every opening. Just as the water bed emptied itself of a massive body of water and flowed into my neighborhood, God poured himself into the body of a human and became flesh in the person of Jesus. All of God became present in the person of Jesus. The Messiah entered the story. God broke absence. The Almighty became present.

Now, not just Israel but all of humanity could leave the dark streets of absence. They could abandon their post, hop across the lawn, and run into their Father's arms. God had made himself present to flood the darkness with light and to push back the encroaching shadows of terror and doubt. "The true light, which gives light to everyone, was coming into the world" (John 1:9).

With Us to Save Us

While all creation was waiting on the edge of the lawn for the Messiah to return, an angel came to a young girl named Mary. Mary was engaged to be married to a man named Joseph, but before the wedding day an angel visited her and told her that she would conceive a child without the help of any man. Gabriel, the angel who visited Mary, began telling her that she would name this boy Jesus and he would be God's Son. When Mary asked how it was possible that she would conceive a child since she was a virgin, Gabriel answered, "The Holy Spirit will come upon you, and the power of the Most High will overshadow you; therefore the child to be born will be called holy—the Son of God" (Luke 1:35).

Here we have the most intense and bewildering moment of God's presence in all of history. God, through his Holy Spirit, became so present with Mary that she conceived a child. We should not read this with any hint of sexuality, but with overt attention to God's condescension. God didn't visit Mary as an incubus—a demon from mythology that engages in sexual activities with unaware sleepers—but used the same power that formed Adam from the dust to pour himself into our world.

Here we have the Son of God in the daughter of woman. Here we have God being present to us in a way never before imagined and never again repeated. God broke all the rules to be present with us. And he came with the name of Jesus.

Jesus means "God saves." God was coming to save. God was becoming present with the world in a new and unchanging way to save the world in a new and unchanging way.[1] He humbled himself to serve. He lowered himself to be lowered further still. He became flesh to save flesh. He would save us from the sin that put separation between us. He would save us from our eternal absence from God.

Now, you have to imagine that this situation would have been desperately confusing for her fiancé, Joseph, so luckily God didn't leave him in the dark either. An angel visited Joseph and told him about God's plan. When the angel explained the story to Joseph, he quoted a very important verse from the Old Testament: "Behold, the virgin shall conceive and bear a son, and they shall call his name Immanuel" (Matt. 1:23). The fulfillment of this prophecy was one of the signs Israel was waiting for. This was the promise that water would run from the hose's mouth. The time had come. The wait was over.

You might be wondering why the prophecy said the virgin's son will be called Immanuel, and yet the baby was named Jesus. This miraculous baby was not given two names, but one name and a title. His name, Jesus, explained what he would do. His title, Immanuel, explained who he was.

Immanuel means "God with us." In light of everything we have seen about the absence of God, the phrase "God with us" should bear a mighty weight. God is not just near us. God is not just generally present. God is not just passing by us as he passed the cleft of the rock. God is not just jiggling the handle of our bedroom door. God is with us. He has come. And the form in which he has come is the most intimate form of presence he could have possibly taken on. God became flesh. God not only was with us once again, but God became like us for the first time in history.

Immanuel means God became an embryo. The inventor of wombs became a fetus. The author of stars became the size of a pen point. The one whose hands hold all things was held inside of Mary. The only being with no beginning had a birthdate. The one whose face we cannot look upon took on the wrinkled skin of a newborn. Presence became personal because presence became a person.

God saves us through Jesus. God is with us through Immanuel. Both of these realities are tied up in the historical man who was born from the Virgin Mary. God is with us to save us. Jesus is Immanuel.

The Word Became Flesh

My wife's favorite holiday is Halloween. However, Halloween seems to be one of the lowest on my list of favorites. She loves this fall holiday for many reasons. The decorations, the pumpkins, the candy, and the kids ringing our doorbell all night fill her with Jack

Skellington–like excitement. But her favorite reason is the most obvious: the costumes.

People get to put on an outfit and become someone else for one evening. When people think about God becoming flesh, they tend to think of it like a long Halloween. God put on the costume of flesh, spent thirty-three years in it, and then shed the outfit so he could go back home. For many people, Immanuel was temporary.

But God with us is anything but temporary. Immanuel is irreversible. There are no take backs when God becomes present to us like he did in Jesus. John 1:14 says, "The Word became flesh." Jesus did not put on flesh or possess a human body. He did not dress up like a human or use one as a temporary vessel. He actually *became* flesh. Flesh became his new nature. This was a permanent change. This was not a thirty-three-year sentence but an eternal transformation. The incarnation of Immanuel was nothing like Halloween.

Stop and think about this for a second. God did not just become present with us; he became present *to* us. He was not just present in the flesh two thousand years ago; he is still present in the flesh today. Jesus sits next to God in heaven, in his glorified human body. This is the same type of body we will have when Jesus returns and glorifies his people.[2]

Jesus is not absent from his human body. His scars from the cross are still present.[3] You do not have a God in heaven who cannot sympathize with you because he has forgotten what it was like to be human.[4] He is human and divine. He became flesh. The presence of God with us is irreversible. That is how near to us God wants to be.

Like my parents' waterbed emptied itself and poured out into the streets, God the Son emptied himself and poured out into flesh. The Word that always was became the Jesus who always is. Listen to this remarkable statement of presence in Colossians 1:19: "In him

[Jesus] all the fullness of God was pleased to dwell." All of God lives in the flesh of Jesus. Hebrews 1:3 states this truth with equal power when it says, "[Jesus] is the radiance of the glory of God and the exact imprint of his nature." That is presence. That is Immanuel. That is a God who longs to be with his people. God is with us. Water is flowing from the hose. The wait is over. Our absent God is finally here.

Jesus Starts at the Bottom

Picture a woman who is about to rappel down the side of a tall cliff. Before taking off down the rock's face, she will first make certain that the rope is long enough to reach the bottom. If the top of the cliff is one hundred feet high, she is going to ensure that she has more than one hundred feet of free rope hanging over the side. In order for her to complete her journey, she has to be able to reach the bottom. If the rope is long enough to reach the mountain's floor, it is sufficient to reach every other part of the journey.

When Jesus left the high cliffs of heaven and came down to earth, he showed us that the rope of his reach is sufficient to reach every single person in the world. By going to the bottom first, Jesus demonstrated that no one is too high or too low for his presence to draw near.

The presence of Jesus with the lowly was evident from his birth. He was not born in a palace fit for a king, let alone fit for the one true God. He was not even born in a place suitable for a child of his parents' meager means. Jesus was born in a stable with the stench of manure and livestock stinging his nostrils. His first crib was a feeding trough. Jesus entered the world as an outcast, as someone absent from the inner circle of society.

God with us looked like nothing the world would have ever

expected. Jesus healed people of life-threatening diseases. He spoke and taught like no one had ever done before. He walked on water and could read people's thoughts. But within Jesus' work and miracles there was a message of presence. His primary sermon was, "Repent, for the kingdom of heaven has come near" (Matt. 4:17 NIV). Not only was God near in the person of Jesus, but he was bringing his kingdom of presence with him. In the way Jesus functioned, there was news of nearness. When God comes to earth, wrongs are made right. Not only did he become close to humanity by becoming flesh, he drew near to the least of humanity to show that no one was outside his reach.

You may think your upbringing was too rough or dirty. You may think your past is too stained with sin and shame. You may have convinced yourself that because of where you came from God could never be present with you. But when we look at the one and only Immanuel, the one and only person who was called "God with us," we see him born at the bottom. There is no length to which God will not go to rescue you from absence. There is no depth to which Jesus will not descend in order to be present with you. God tested his rope to make sure it was long enough to reach the bottom, and he succeeded when he was born as a baby in a slop trough.

The life of Jesus was also an example of his nearness and presence with the outcasts of society. Jesus did not engage in trickle-down ministry. He did not go first to the kings and the rulers, working his way down the ladder of importance. Neither did Jesus just go to those lower in the social pyramid. He became present with those whom everyone else was absent from, regardless of their position in society.

Those suffering from the disease of leprosy—one of the most vile and contagious ailments of Jesus' time—were quarantined off from the rest of society. No one went near them until God did. For the ill, the deformed, the unwanted, and the infectious, Jesus was Immanuel. Those living lives unfit for everyday life were scorned and neglected as second-rate, much like they are today. Prostitutes were untouchables, since to be seen with them would put you in suspicion of fornication. But Jesus spent time with prostitutes. For the sex workers, drug dealers, and smut peddlers, Jesus was Immanuel.

These people were not God's side mission but his main mission. Listen to the words from the Old Testament that Jesus read in the temple and applied to himself in Luke 4:18: "The Spirit of the Lord is upon me, because he has anointed me to proclaim good news to the poor. He has sent me to proclaim liberty to the captives and recovering of sight to the blind, to set at liberty those who are oppressed."

God came to be with the homeless who live in poverty. The one who sees all took on mortal eyes so that he could put his healing hands on the blind. The only truly free being in the universe bound himself under oppressive skin so that he could set free those under tyranny.

This liberating presence of Jesus applies to all of us. We are all poor, for we do not have the riches of God's righteousness. We are all imprisoned by our shackles of sin and mortality. We are all utterly blind, for we cannot see the truth or our Creator. And we are all severely oppressed by our ever-looming and inevitable death.

Jesus is our Savior. He came to set us free. By going to the lowest of the low and the neediest of the needy, Jesus showed us that there is no amount of absence we can heap upon ourselves that his presence cannot pierce. For the whole world, from bottom to top, Jesus is our Immanuel.

Veiled Jesus

But despite all he did, not everyone saw Jesus as God. When some people looked at Jesus, they did not see God. That is the shocking part of the "Word became flesh" passage. John 1:9–11 says,

"The true light, which gives light to everyone, was coming into the world. He was in the world, and the world was made through him, yet the world did not know him. He came to his own, and his own people did not receive him."

Jesus is the ultimate reality to which Moses's cleft in the rock pointed. For that split in the rock both revealed and concealed the glory of God. It gave Moses a window through which to see the radiance of the Father but also limited his view so that he could not perceive the full splendor of the one true God. The same is true for Jesus. God is both revealed and concealed in the person of Immanuel. He is fully revealed in Jesus since "in him all the fullness of God was pleased to dwell."[5] But Jesus is also the concealed image of God. Unless we apprehend him by faith we cannot see the glory of God that resides in him. In fact, Jesus said the very purpose of some of his parables was that some "may indeed see but not perceive, and may indeed hear but not understand."[6] In Jesus we find the final word on presence and absence for those who would receive him and those who would reject him. To those who would receive him, he is more present than ever. To those who would reject him, even his most radical nearness is complete absence.

This misapprehension of presence is like a father who has been away at war a long time. He left his wife and three young girls behind and fought for eight long years in four different countries. Every week he would send letters home to his family. Sometimes he would address love letters to his wife, pouring out intimate longings and reminiscing about shared memories. Other times he would address them to each of his three children collectively or individually. The letters would tell them what he was doing, how he wished he could see how they had grown, and, most of all, how much he loved them.

The father ached with a longing to be present with his family, and his family ached with a longing to be present with their father. Finally, after nearly a decade of fighting abroad, the father journeys home. Wearing his freshly pressed uniform and removing his army green cap from his newly cut head of hair, the father knocks on his family's door.

His youngest daughter opens the door and says, "Can I help you?" The father tears up and bends down to embrace his daughter. The little girl screams in fear and runs away, crying, "Mommy! Mommy!"

The mother comes to the door with the three children standing behind her. "Is there something I can do for you, sir?" she asks.

The father is stunned. "It's me, your husband. Hey, girls, it's me, your father. I've come back from the war. Don't you recognize me? I've traveled so far to see you."

The family stares blankly at him. Finally, his wife speaks up. "We have been getting letters for eight years from my husband and the father of my children. He has explained his journeys, his feelings, and his coming. You are not the man we have been expecting from these letters. You are not my husband, nor are you the father of my children. Good day." With that, the wife closes the door, leaving the husband alone on the porch.

The ravages of war had taken such a toll on this soldier that even his wife could no longer recognize that the man she had married was standing right in front of her. This is similar to how people perceived Jesus. God had come to the world, and the world did not recognize him. God had been sending letters for thousands of years, telling his people about his happenings, his love, and his coming. But when he came, Jesus did not match the expectations of his family. God was veiled because he did not look like what the world was expecting. Our false understanding of Jesus is one way in which we still experience absence today.

Absence in Misunderstanding

There is a famous story in John 6 in which Jesus feeds more than five thousand people with only fives loaves of bread and two fish. After the massive crowd experienced this miracle, they realized that this man was someone special. Jesus must be the one God had written about in the law and the prophets. But they misunderstood what Jesus was on earth to do. They decided that they were going to set up Jesus as their earthly king.

The crowd knew what they wanted their God to be like, and they would force him into that image whether he liked it or not. But before the crowd could do anything to force Jesus into a position of earthly power, he withdrew. Jesus became absent. When man tries to make God into something he is not, God withdraws.

This idea became hauntingly clear to me one night outside a Starbucks in Southern California. It was a warm summer night, and I was doing some reading underneath one of those iconic green umbrellas. After an hour or so, a man in his late twenties asked what I was reading. Since it was a Christian book, we struck up a conversation about the church and about his problems with it. Growing up Catholic and now mostly affiliated with some offshoot of Buddhism, this man had some strange and unique views. However unfounded most of them were, he did have one insight that shook me to my core so much that I will never forget it.

After about thirty minutes of discussing the differences between who Jesus really was and what his Christians are like today, this man said in a completely serious tone, "Sometimes I wonder if the Antichrist is the Jesus your churches have invented." Upon asking several questions to get him to flesh out such a harsh statement, I discovered what he meant. He was saying that in many of our churches, we have formed Jesus in our own image.

We want a Jesus who accepts the life we like to live. So we attend churches that don't dig too deeply into our personal lives. We want a Jesus who is full of love. So we blot out all teachings of hell, sin, justification, and repentance from the pulpit. We want a Jesus who blesses us with material goods. So we surround ourselves with teaching about the good gifts of God and shut our ears to the calls for sacrificial giving. When we form Jesus into our own image, he is not Jesus. He is an anti-Jesus. When we make an idol of Jesus in our image present, Immanuel may become absent.

Making Jesus into our own image does not bring him closer but drives him away. The crowd of five thousand wanted God to be present in a different way. They wanted God to be the conquering king who would take the throne and slay their enemies. We, too, want God to be present in different ways.

We want him to be nearer than he is. We want to see more of his glory than we see. We want to stand in his immediate presence more than we can now. But we must understand that even in Jesus, God was still hidden. Even in the presence of Jesus, there was a measure of absence. Even in Immanuel, God is absent in the way we most desire but present in the way we most require. God was veiled in Jesus, but Jesus had a plan to tear the veil.

TWELVE

PRESENT FOR ABSENCE

How did Jesus defeat absence?

And he put all things under his feet and gave
him as head over all things to the church, which
is his body, the fullness of him who fills all in all.
—EPHESIANS 1:22–23

I was born and raised in Oklahoma City. As an OKC native, the bombing of the Murrah Building on April 19, 1995, has always been a distinct memory of mine. I was in the first grade when Timothy McVeigh and Terry Nichols drove a five-hundred-pound bomb of mixed chemicals directly beneath the day care center of a government multiplex called the Alfred P. Murrah Federal Building.

At 9:02 in the morning, my classroom, twenty miles away from the blast zone, shook violently as the detonation rattled

throughout the entire metro area. The eruption destroyed or dam-
aged 582 buildings, caused $652 million worth of damage, injured
680 people, and took the lives of 168 humans beings—including
3 pregnant women and 19 children. My city was in turmoil.

What followed was one of the most impassioned cries for justice to ever ring through the court systems of our country. People
from all over the world, not just Oklahoma, were calling for these
men's lives. Justice was what they demanded. Retribution was what
they cried for. They insisted that these men be held responsible for
what they had done.

A desire for justice is part of what it means to be a human being.
Since God is just, and we are made in his image, we yearn for justice
along with him. Even when we were young this was true. When our
pencil got stolen in elementary school, or our little sister got shoved
to the asphalt on the playground, we would run to our teachers and
demand that something be done about it. So when something as
big as the Murrah bombing happens, collective humanity screams
for justice.

Now imagine that the two convicted criminals, Timothy
McVeigh and Terry Nichols, are sitting in the courtroom await-
ing their sentences. All the proof has been gathered, all the guilt
has been laid, and all the confessions have been made. There is no
doubt that these two men are responsible for the tragedy that hit
OKC back in 1995. The two defendants can hear the faint yells of
protesters seeping through the courthouse doors, demanding their
execution or life in prison.

The judge looks at the two criminals and says, "I know what
you have done. All the evidence is here, and it is conclusive that you
are guilty. Everyone agrees that you both deserve to die." The judge
picks up his gavel and cocks his wrist, indicating that he is about to
slam it down with his punishment. With a brassy clear voice and

the wood-on-wood clap of his hammer, the judge says, "I find you not guilty. You are cleared of all charges and are free to go."

What would be the response of Oklahomans? What would have been the response of this world? Would we have fawned over the judge, calling him kind, loving, forgiving, long-suffering, and merciful? No! We would be furious. We would call the judge a crook, an evil and corrupt man. Only a judge who gives justice is good.

This is the same situation we are in with God. We have committed a crime against the eternal law of the eternal God. Though we could never tally up the damage our sins have done, like the dollars and casualties of the Murrah bombing, God knows how many people we've hurt and how many hearts we've scarred.

No matter how dire a tragedy committed on earth is, it is far less compared to what it means to violate the will of the only good and perfect Creator. Nevertheless, we want God to pardon us. We want to go into God's court, as guilty as the bombers of the Murrah Building, and hear, "You are free to go."

Why does God get held to a lesser standard than our earthly judges? Shouldn't he, of all judges, be held to the highest authority? If God didn't repay with justice every wrong committed, he would no longer be good. If God was no longer good, he would no longer be our God. For the God of the Bible is always good and just, repaying everyone for their deeds.[1] But we are not the only ones who want the words "You are free to go" to come out of God's mouth.

God himself wishes to speak them to us because he loves us so much. This is why Jesus had to come to earth. Someone innocent must receive all the punishment that we deserved. Since none of us were qualified for this position, God had to fulfill it himself. We were so absent from God that we could never be present with him. So God became present to us in order that he could take on the absence we deserved.

Present in the Passion

Jesus knew this was his mission. Even though his earthly brain was no different from any other human being's, his mind was bent on God's will. Immanuel knew that he was with us to die. Jesus made this clear to his disciples multiple times, even though they had trouble believing it. As Matthew 16:21 says, "Jesus began to explain to his disciples that he must go to Jerusalem and suffer many things at the hands of the elders, the chief priests and the teachers of the law, and that he must be killed and on the third day be raised to life" (NIV). Jesus became present to die for our absence.

That's why it was no surprise to Jesus when one of his own disciples, Judas, handed him over to the high priest and a well-armed mob. It was no surprise to Jesus when he was mocked and beaten while being held in custody. It was no surprise to Jesus that the people he came to save would chant "Crucify him" in the courts of Pilate. It was no surprise to Jesus that he was whipped, crowned with thorns, stripped of his clothes, strapped to Rome's cruelest instrument of death, and led outside of the city to die.

It was no surprise to Jesus because it was what he came to earth to do, and he was present for every horrible second of it. When the Word became flesh, he received all the same nerve endings, pain thresholds, and vulnerability that we have. When he hammered his thumb while working as a carpenter, it hurt just as badly as when we do it at home. Jesus being God with us meant that he was vulnerable. Jesus was exposed to pain, exhaustion, bleeding out, suffocation, and dehydration. But through all Jesus endured, he never made himself absent. Jesus was present through every trial he bore.

When Pilate sentenced him to be flogged, Jesus did not use some kind of power to escape from his body while the torture proceeded. He was present in his vulnerable body for every gash of the flog.

Even as the triad of leather ropes, dangling with sharp bone from their nine tails, buried themselves in Immanuel's back, he never stopped being God with us. When the more than one-hundred-pound crossbeam was placed on Jesus' back, he was present to lumber it out of the city gates and up to the hilltop of his execution.

When he was fastened on the wooden cross, Jesus was present to feel the iron nails puncture his skin, tissue, muscle, and bone. When the cross was raised up, Jesus had to push against the nails in his feet and hands in order to give his lungs the room necessary to take in a breath, and he was present for every single inhalation. For six hours, Jesus was on the cross.

If Jesus only breathed once a minute, he would still have had to go through this lifting and breathing ritual three hundred and sixty times. There have been plenty of movies made about the crucifixion of Jesus, but no director has had the time to show the full length that Jesus spent on the cross. But Immanuel endured every second of it.

Jesus was completely present in his suffering so that he would not be absent in ours. We can go through no pain, no loss, no hurt, no persecution that Jesus did not feel with his own skin and nerves. If you feel like you are going through something so terrible that God cannot be sympathetic to it, remember the cross. Remember that you are not alone, writhing in absence. The Word became flesh so that his flesh could feel what you are going through. He is present in your pain, for he has borne it himself.

These moments of suffering are the door to the courthouse through which Jesus had to enter in order to stand in our place. We were the ones who deserved the public ridicule, but he was present in our place. We were the ones who had earned brutal scourging for our crimes, but he was present in our place. We were the ones who had piled up a list of grievances that earned for us the one-hundred-pound crossbeam, but he was present in our place. We were the ones who broke the eternal law of the eternal God and deserved to be hanged out until we died, but he was present in our place. Jesus is Immanuel—God with us and God for us.

Justice

Most people are uncomfortable with talking about Jesus in this way. If the discomfort comes from a place of empathy or sadness, then that is most likely a good type of discomfort. But a lot of the uncomfortable feelings we have are about the cross itself. Do we really need all the pain and torture? What's the point of explaining everything Jesus went through? Does it make a difference if he suffered much or only a little? Why do we need all this blood?

When I first started to think about blood and sacrifices, I was a little put off by it. The idea seemed archaic, old, and barbaric. I was reminded of a haunting scene from the movie *Apocalypto* in which an ancient civilization commits human sacrifices on top of a massive altar in order to appease their fictitious gods. Blood made Christianity seem wrong. Blood made Christianity seem man-made.

But it was not man who came up with the idea for blood. God gave us blood to be the means of our forgiveness. We see it exampled after the first sin, when God shed the blood of animals to clothe Adam and Eve.[2] We also see it explained when God gave Moses the law: "For the life of a creature is in the blood, and I have given it to you to make atonement for yourselves on the altar; it is the blood that makes atonement for one's life" (Lev. 17:11 NIV).

Blood was God's plan all along. Blood represents life. When blood is shed, life ends. That is why blood makes atonement. One life is forfeit; another life is sacrificed instead. Blood is the means God gave for forgiveness.

However, the blood of animals would never be enough to properly display the holiness of God. Hebrews 10:4 tells us, "It is impossible for the blood of bulls and goats to take away sins." Animal sacrifices were for a season. They could not make a way for man to be present with God. Man had to be punished for sin. Flesh for flesh. The problem was, there was no innocent party to put the sin on. That is why the Word had to become flesh.

The Word became flesh so that he could have veins. God became man so that his heart could pump blood. God let blood become his life force so that he could shed it for us.

God wants to be present with us. This desire is held in tension between two competing caricatures of God. On the one hand, we have to ask, How can God draw near to us without destroying us? How can God be present in all his holiness without making the unholy completely absent? On the other hand, we have to ask, How can God show us his love and grace without giving up his justice? How can God forgive us without acting like sin is no big deal? How can he express his holiness without consuming us, and his love without condoning our sins? How can the nail go into the power outlet without killing the child or turning off the electricity?

Some people see God as cruel, vindictive, and harsh. They think he is a judge and a judge only, that he is the playground bully who punishes all who stand opposed to his trifles. On the other side of the spectrum we have those who see God as only the God of love. They view him as an indulgent father who will sacrifice and compromise anything for the sake of his people. Their God is the divine with no spine. This God does not judge or condemn because he would rather love. But properly understanding God's presence on the cross saves us from these caricatures.

The presence of Jesus solves this riddle for us. In order for God to show us his holiness, sin must be punished. In order for God to show us his grace, he must take the punishment. God displayed his justice by pouring out his wrath on Jesus. God displayed his love by being the One on whom he poured out his wrath. We must not look at the Father as the Judge and the Son as the Savior. It is the same God who saves us through Christ from and for himself. This is how God is able to be, as Paul said, "just and the justifier" (Rom. 3:26).

Why Have You Forsaken Me?

The justice people called for after the Murrah bombing in OKC was only partial justice. In fact, all the justice our court systems can provide is partial. Judges can send a guilty man to his death or put him in prison for the rest of his life, but no judge can reverse what the guilty man did. No matter what penalty the judges placed on Timothy McVeigh and Terry Nichols, not one of the victims would stop being dead. Not one of the families who lost a loved one would instantly have them back at home. Not one of the children who perished would be given the opportunity to reach an old age. Wrath could be poured out on McVeigh and Nichols, but the absence of those who died could not be overcome by a judge's sentence.

Jesus is better than our judges. God does not offer partial justice. He does not solve 99 percent of the problem. Jesus did not come just to take our wrath but our absence. He did not take only our punishment but our position. What Jesus endured on the cross earned for us a comprehensive restoration. It would be like the sentencing of the guilty bombers resurrecting every victim, healing every wound, repairing every broken window, and restoring every soul. God poured out his full justice, of both wrath and absence, onto Jesus so that we might have both forgiveness and presence.

Since God is so holy and we are so sinful, we deserve to be absent from him forever. All we have earned with our lives is the right to be cut off from every good thing that comes from God and receive the just wrath that flows out of his holiness. But Jesus became absent from God for us.

After hours and hours of hanging on the cross, being fully present in every moment, Jesus cried out, "My God, my God, why have you forsaken me?" (Matt. 27:46). This is almost unfathomable. The Word who existed in eternity past with God, the uncreated, ever-living Son of God, was now forsaken by God. He who had unending, perfect communion was now experiencing the agonizing pain of God's wrath and absence. The perfect Lamb was held guilty for the sins of the world. God the Son was absent from God.

You and I experience only a miniature level of absence compared to what Jesus endured on the cross. God is still present with us in his general presence. Even if he is absent in the way we most desire, he is still present in the way we most require. Our lives still have good things in them, even if they are few, and God is the provider of all of them.

Our souls do not know and our minds cannot comprehend the incommunicable pain of what entering into God's full absence feels like. It is like lungs not getting oxygen. It is like the heart not getting blood. We were created in God's image, and having that image ripped away from us is absolutely unbearable. Yet this is what Jesus went through for us, and on an infinitely greater scale.

The words Jesus cried out on the cross are quoted from Psalm 22. When Jesus said those few words from the cross, he was communicating the weight and absence expressed by this song of sorrow. David wrote, "Why are you so far from saving me?" (v. 1), but Jesus became condemned so that we would be saved.

David wrote, "Be not far from me" (v. 11), but God was as far as he could be from Jesus.

David wrote, "O LORD, do not be far off! O you my help, come quickly to my aid!" (v. 19). But God was far off, and no aid came to Jesus as his life faded on the cross.

Jesus not only bore the punishment our flesh deserves, he bore the punishment our souls deserve. For we do not just deserve death, but we deserve separation. Jesus was given over to absence so that we could experience presence. Jesus endured utter darkness so we could step into the light. Jesus was cast off so we could be taken in. Jesus was abandoned so we could be accepted. His presence healed our absence. His absence earned our presence.

Perhaps 1 Peter 3:18 says it best, "For Christ also suffered once for sins, the righteous for the unrighteous, that he might bring us to God." The good news of the gospel is that we get God!

The Veil

It's baffling to think that while Jesus was on the cross, other Israelites were having a normal day. Mothers could be seen buying grain and fruit from the local marketplace in preparation for the coming Sabbath. The city gates were abuzz with the comings and goings of travelers in town for the huge celebration of Passover. The temple would have been the focal point for all the happenings of Jerusalem during this time of year.

There were three main sections in the temple where Israel brought their sacrifices of atonement. There was the outer court, the inner court, and the Holy of Holies. The outer court was as close to the temple as women were allowed to get. The inner court was separated into more sections. Some of the sections allowed all the Israelite men. Others required priesthood to enter.

But there was a final, innermost part of the temple that only the high priest could enter once a year. This was the Holy of Holies. This is where the incomprehensible amalgamation of God's special, visible, and actual presence dwelled. In order to get to this inner sanctuary, the high priest had to pass through all sorts of tables, altars, and washing basins. But most significantly, he had to pass through a thick curtain, or a veil.

The veil separated God's presence from the rest of the world. God was inside. The world was outside. God was present in the Holy of Holies. The world was absent in the outer courts and beyond.

When Jesus died on the cross, however, something miraculous happened inside the belly of the temple. After Jesus said, "It is finished" (John 19:30) and gave up his last breath, the veil that stood outside the Holy of Holies was supernaturally ripped from top to bottom.[3] God's presence was won for the world by the sacrifice of Jesus. Now that Jesus' atoning blood had been shed, mankind had a way to be present with the holy God. Mankind used to need priests, temples, rituals, and sacrifices to enter into God's presence. But now, all we need is Jesus.

Hebrews 6:19–20 expresses what was happening here in beautiful language. The author was trying to explain the certainty we have in our hope in God's promises. He wrote, "We have this as a sure and steadfast anchor of the soul, a hope that enters into the inner place behind the curtain, where Jesus has gone as a forerunner on our behalf."

Jesus is our forerunner. Jesus, through his death, has gone ahead of us into God's innermost presence. We are now following after him, through the curtain, into God's glorious presence.

Because Jesus experienced God's absence, now we don't have to. Because Jesus entered God's presence, now we get to.[4]

Our hope is not a wild guess. We're not placing bets on a craps table, hoping the dice fall the right way. We have a guarantee that we will enter into God's presence. That guarantee is the resurrection of Jesus.

The Dual Hope and Longing in the Resurrection

On the cross, Immanuel died. God with us died for us. The Word that became flesh laid it down. Can you imagine the turmoil and confusion of Jesus' disciples? For those who followed Jesus through his ministry, this death on the cross must have looked like proof positive that he was merely a prophet and not the divine presence for which they had been waiting. The God who came was now dead. The One who was present was now absent.

But Jesus did not remain absent. The Word that became flesh and died became the Savior who rose again and was glorified. Jesus rose from the grave. In his resurrection, he didn't make himself absent from his flesh, but put on a glorified human body. He conquered death, and his presence returned. The resurrection of Jesus is the essential truth of the Christian faith. Without it, Paul said we who are Christians are to be pitied above all men.[5]

The event of God raising Jesus from the dead is so central to the Christian faith because it is our guarantee that Jesus is who he said he was and that he has the power to accomplish that which he promised he would accomplish. God validated Jesus by vindicating him from the grave. In the raising of Christ, all the claims, promises, and teachings of Jesus found their irrevocable stamp of truth.

Since God raised Jesus from the grave, we can be assured that we who are in him will be raised just as he was.[6] The claim that Jesus' death bore our sin and condemnation is made true in his resurrection. In short, the fact that Jesus came out of that tomb guarantees our future with God. All the promises made about our future are concretely sealed in the resurrection.

Think of it this way. My wife and I lived in the Philippines for several months, helping the poor reach self-sufficiency by giving them free goats. Along with the rest of the goat team, we would talk to people in need every day about our program and the benefits of raising goats. Once they were somewhat excited about the idea of having goats of their own, we would tell them that we wanted to give them several goats for free. You can imagine that they were skeptical.

In an attempt to assuage their fears, we would tell them about the other villages in which we had given goats, we would show them pictures of other happy families we had worked with, and we would share with them our extensive knowledge about goat raising. However, many of the people were still very doubtful that we were actually just going to give them goats for free.

After they agreed to raising goats, we would offer some extensive education about care, feeding, safety, medication, and how to best make a living off of a goat. Once all our preliminary checks were in order, we would move on to step two. And it is in this step that all their doubts would fade away.

My wife and I, along with a few of our Filipino friends, would hop in our tiny purple Mitsubishi truck and head to the hardware store to buy everything we needed for a proper goat house. Now, when I say "hardware store," I don't mean an Ace Hardware or Lowe's. I mean a field full of two by fours, palm leaves, and bamboo. We would get all the supplies we needed and load them into our tiny truck.

Oftentimes the bounty was so rich that we had to have some-one drive behind us on a dirt bike to hold loose bits of lumber that were dangling off the back of our short-bedded vehicle. With construction materials in tow, we would pull into our soon-to-be-goat-owner's village. And you can only imagine the looks on their faces. Disbelief, wonder, and joy filled these families' whole expressions as what we promised began to seem more real. And as we took up hammer, nail, and palm branches, side by side with our new Filipino friends, to build their goat houses, that which we promised was guaranteed. When they looked at all the work we did for them, the supplies we bought, and the amount of care we put into building their new goat house, they knew beyond a shadow of a doubt that they would become goat owners.

This is a tiny picture of what the resurrection of Jesus is like to us. Jesus promised us eternal life, forgiveness of sins, and an endless dwelling place in the presence of God. But, like free goats to a poor family in the Philippines, these things sounded a little too good to be true. It wasn't until God raised Jesus from the dead that all his promises became a guarantee. Just like the goat house offered assurance to the families to whom we promised goats, the resurrection of Jesus offers assurance to those of us to whom he has promised life.

There is one more element to the story that is worth noting. The families still did not have their goats. The house had to be built first. Then we had to go buy the goats, vaccinate them, and ensure they were healthy before we could place them in their new home. The goats were absent! The hope was real. The promise was real. The guarantee was unshakable. But the goats were absent. They were in the future. They still had to be waited on. They were forthcoming.

This is where our hope lies. The closest, most present, nearest hope we have for our future is tied up in the raising of Jesus from the dead. But the resurrection of Jesus also meant his ascension, his going back up into heaven. And the ascension of Jesus also meant his bodily absence from the world. Though we are told it is better that he left so that we may receive the Holy Spirit (a truth that we must not overlook, and one that will be discussed in the next chapter), we are still left without the physical Christ in this world.

Furthermore, the consummation of many of the promises that Jesus came to bring us are still postponed for the future. God came near but is still far. God came to our present but remains in our future. God guaranteed our presence with him when he came near but left us with hope and longing when he left. Jesus is present in one sense and absent in another.

The apostle Paul said this best in Romans 8:22–24: "For we know that the whole creation has been groaning together in the pains of childbirth until now. And not only the creation, but we ourselves, who have the firstfruits of the Spirit, groan inwardly as we wait eagerly for adoption as sons, the redemption of our bodies. For in this hope we were saved."

We are groaning in pain for Jesus to return. We are eagerly waiting on tiptoes for Jesus to come and transform our bodies to be like his new heavenly body. We have a sure hope, but it is still a hope in what is to come.

Therefore, the resurrection of Jesus leaves the Christian in a victorious and assured state, yet one that is slightly ironic. Because he who came as a fulfillment of the Old Testament fulfilled it by prolonging its fulfillment. In the resurrection we have both assurance and waiting, possession and longing. We are an ironic people. We can say, in the same breath, God has come near and God is still far. We can say without any contradiction that Jesus is present and Jesus is absent. We can hold without any amount of falsehood that our hope is made secure in the resurrection of Jesus and our longing is made greater in that same resurrection.

Jesus Is Our Presence

Jesus earned what we could never earn: entry into the glorious presence of God. Throughout our entire lives and our entire history, all we have ever done is earn absence. Jesus is the antidote to absence.

Jesus brings resolution and fulfillment to all the absence we have struggled to overcome. Just as God shed animal blood to clothe Adam and Eve in new garments, Jesus shed his blood to clothe us in himself. Just as the aroma of God's general presence fills our bellies with hunger, like we have just smelled freshly baked bread, Jesus is the Bread of Life we actually get to feast on. Just as God put Moses in the cleft of the rock to shield him from the full blast of his glory, Jesus is the rock in which we are hidden from all our past mistakes. Just as God called Abraham to be absent to his homeland so that he could be present in his new home, Jesus has called us out of our homes and has gone to prepare a place for us to be present with him.

Just as Solomon came for his wife, Jesus has come, with great love, for us. Just as Israel sought out God in the temple, Jesus brought the presence of God to us in the temple of his very body. Job suffered in the presence of God, but Jesus suffered in the absence of God so that we could live in his presence. Just as Jonah was regurgitated out of the belly of the fish, Jesus' resurrection has earned us a way out of the mouth of the grave.

Jesus is always Immanuel. From before he was born, "God with us" was his name.[7] Before leaving earth, Jesus promised that Immanuel would never go away when he said, "I am with you always, to the end of the age."[8] Jesus is always Immanuel.

The absence that threatened to swallow us up like the grave has been conquered by the death, burial, and resurrection of Jesus. The justice we deserved was given to Jesus on the cross. The separation we earned was placed between God and his Son while he died in our place. The absence we should suffer for eternity was suffered by Christ on our behalf. Because Jesus was separated, we get to be reunited. Through the death and resurrection of Christ, we can enter through the veil. He became our absence. He earned our presence.

THIRTEEN

THE SPIRIT AND ABSENCE

Is God absent if he lives in me?

*I will put my Spirit within you, and cause
you to walk in my statutes and be careful to
obey my rules. You shall dwell in the land
that I gave to your fathers, and you shall
be my people, and I will be your God.*
—Ezekiel 36:27–28

When I was about four years old, my house got a new toilet.
To this day I have no idea why, but the new bathroom
fixture enthralled me. After trying it out for the first time, my
family and I went over to my grandparents' house. I ran into the
house, found my granddad, and exclaimed, "We got a new stoilet
stool!" My granddad thought this was the funniest thing he had
ever heard.

My granddad was one of the most joyful and whimsical men I've ever known. Almost every time I saw him, he'd sing me the Davy Crockett theme song—since that was his affectionate nickname for me—and recount to me the "stoilet stool" episode. He loved joking around and retelling old stories. He was seldom serious and rarely reserved. Which is why it was so odd that he was in the insurance business. Earl was his name, and he was as much of a smart businessman as he was a jokester.

My grandfather opened up a modest mutual fund for every single one of his grandchildren. When I was about ten, he sat me down and explained how the investment account worked. "You see, Davy Crockett," he began, "investing requires sacrifice. In order for you to have a mutual fund, you have to sacrifice some of your money." I nodded my head but clearly not convincingly enough. So my patient granddad grabbed a five-dollar bill out of his billfold and held it out to me. I took it happily.

My young mind began racing with what I could buy with that five dollars. I could get a pack of trading cards, a new Tech Deck, or a whole mess of candy. As I took the bill from my granddad, he told me to put it in my pocket. I greedily obeyed. He said, "You now have five dollars in your pocket. That is your money. Now, let's say you wanted to invest that money by opening up a mutual fund like I did for you."

So far I was tracking with him. "In order for you to have a mutual fund, you have to say good-bye to the five dollars you already have." He leveled his palm out like a table and raised one eyebrow. I wasn't too keen on the idea of giving him my recently acquired cash. And although this lesson was costing me five bucks, I went with it.

As I put the five-dollar bill in his hand, he took it and continued, "Now you don't have five dollars anymore. In fact, since this is a mutual fund like the one I opened for you, you won't be able to touch this five dollars until you are twenty-one years old." Now he had gone too far. I thought he was going to do a trick like magicians do when they ask for a volunteer's money. They make you feel like you've lost it before bringing it back safe and sound from behind your ear. But I didn't want to wait more than a decade to get my five bucks back.

Apparently my granddad could see my frustration. He said, "But here's the best part. When you do turn twenty-one, you won't just get your five dollars back, you'll get this back." With that he pulled a brand-new one-hundred-dollar bill out of his wallet. That crisp, just from the bank note was the first Benjamin I had come face-to-face with. My five dollars seemed like an old discarded Christmas toy from four years ago compared to this newfound treasure. I wanted it. "I know it's hard to say good-bye to your five dollars now," my granddad told me, "but a mutual fund is a guarantee of a future reward. It's worth saying good-bye to a little so you can say hello to a lot."

My five dollars may have been absent from my pocket, but I knew two things that comforted me: my mutual fund was present and I had a reward coming. The five dollars was realer to me and far more tactile, but I had something new: an account guaranteeing a future of more.

This is similar to the absence of Jesus and the presence of the Holy Spirit. Jesus had to leave the earth so that the Holy Spirit could come. Before going to the cross, Jesus said to his disciples, "I am going to him who sent me. . . . It is to your advantage that I go away, for if I do not go away, the Helper will not come to you. But if I go, I will send him to you" (John 16:5, 7).

When Jesus left the earth to return to heaven, it was like giving my granddad the five dollars. The money I had was absent to me. Jesus was absent to the earth. But something was earned from the absence. For my five dollars, it was the mutual fund. For the risen Christ, it was the Holy Spirit—more presence. And just as my mutual fund guaranteed a future reward greater than the original deposit, so does the Holy Spirit in us guarantee a future reward when Jesus returns in glory. Jesus gives us more of God's presence through the Holy Spirit and promises that more is to come.

The absence of the Son means the advent of the Spirit. The leaving of Jesus means the coming of the Ghost. Though the Spirit is a mark of amazing presence, it is also the signal of a new form of absence. God is present in the way we most require in his Spirit but absent in the way we most desire in his person. But, as Jesus promised, this divine swap would be for the benefit of his followers.

The Coming of the Spirit

The absence of the Son of God did not seem beneficial to Jesus' disciples at first. They were already a fearful and confused bunch of followers while Jesus was on earth. When Jesus was arrested and taken to the cross, most of the disciples scattered. They hid, denied Jesus, and lost all hope. When Jesus was taken from the disciples, their spirits failed within them. When Jesus died on the cross, their souls were crushed. When he rose from the grave, they were wildly excited, but when Jesus ascended into heaven, leaving them behind, the disciples waited in the upper room of a house for this promised Spirit to come.

While the disciples were waiting in the Upper Room, the festival of Pentecost was happening outside. *Pentecost* means "the fiftieth day." Fifty days after the Passover, which was the day of Jesus' death, Pentecost was honored to celebrate God giving the

Law to Moses on Mount Sinai. There is great significance in these two Jewish holidays and what occurred on them in the days of the New Testament.

Jesus died on Passover. The holiday of Passover was a time for the Jews to remember when the angel of death passed over their homes in Egypt. God had instructed all the Hebrew families to spread blood from the Passover lamb on the outside of their door and promised that if they did, their household would be spared from the death of their firstborn. Jesus is now our Passover Lamb. For those who believe in Jesus, his blood is spread over the door of our lives, and God's wrath passes over us, sparing us from death. Jesus is the ultimate Passover Lamb whose blood saves us, and he is the firstborn Son who died when we deserved to.

Pentecost was also a remarkably appropriate date for the coming of the promised Holy Spirit. During Pentecost, the people of Israel remembered the day when God gave Moses the Law. Before Jesus, all the Jews had to help them live according to God's will was the Law, and they constantly failed at keeping it. However, on the day of Pentecost, while the disciples were in the Upper Room, what the prophet Ezekiel spoke came true:

> I will give you a new heart and put a new spirit in you; I will remove from you your heart of stone and give you a heart of flesh. And I will put my Spirit in you and move you to follow my decrees and be careful to keep my laws. (Ezek. 36:26–27 NIV)

The Spirit of God came down upon the disciples. He gave them a new heart and moved them to obey God's will. The coming of the Spirit was not like the coming of the Law. The Law brought a list of rules that no human was ever able to fully obey. The Spirit brought a freedom that enabled humans to obey. The Spirit did not bring a new law outside the lives of the disciples. The Spirit embedded a new heart inside the disciples. And this heart moved them to action.

The disciples were transformed. Those fearful, flip-flopping, feet-dragging disciples became champions of the church. They stood unflinching under violent persecution. They spoke up before mobs and kings. They spread the gospel of their risen Jesus across the face of the inhabited world. They even suffered to the point of death for what they believed.

What was the difference between the fearful disciples hiding after Jesus' arrest and the bold disciples dying after Jesus' ascension? The difference was the Holy Spirit. The Spirit of God empowered them in a mighty new way. Jesus was right when he said it would be to their benefit that he left. Following Jesus now had power behind it because it had God within it. God wasn't in the temple; he was within his people.

New Temples

When I set out to buy my wife an engagement ring, I was pretty broke. I was working as a part-time youth minister at a church of about fifty people while getting my undergraduate degree in Bible. I remember going to the jewelry store for the first time. I chose the nicest jewelry store in town. They had security guards at the door, a crystal chandelier on the ceiling, and a high-end stash of secret jewelry for invited guests only.

I made my way up to one of the display cases and put my sweaty hands on the glass. I looked with wonder at all the shining rocks, cast in brilliant yellow and white gold. All the different cuts, sizes, colors, and purities astounded me. These rings were present to me in a way but inaccessible to me at the moment.

That was until an employee strolled over to me and asked if he could help me. He wanted to know what I was looking for and what my price range was. After hearing my budget, he informed me that I would be better off at one of the chain jewelry stores. I didn't have nearly enough money to purchase even their most modest ring. Now these jewels really were inaccessible to me. I could not pay a high enough price to get behind the secure glass case and make one of the rings my own.

Israel had a similar relationship with God in the temple. The presence of God was sealed off in the secure area of the Holy of Holies. Even though the temple was a place of special presence, it represented and perpetuated an age of absence. God was sectioned off and isolated from access. Instead of a glass case, the Holy of Holies had a thick veil that kept everyone except the high priest out. The high priest did not come into the jewelry store of God's presence like a high roller, able to purchase whatever he wanted. He came in like the employee, cleaning the rings and keeping everyone else out.

But imagine if, while I am being turned away from those expensive rings, a lavishly rich man comes into the jewelry store. In a loud voice he announces that he will buy every ring in the store. He instructs the workers to remove the glass tops from the cases and allow everyone in the store to pick whatever rings they want. This man is able to pay a high enough price to make that which was inaccessible more accessible than it has ever been.

This is what Jesus did for us on the cross. God's presence was inaccessible, but he paid the high price of his perfect blood to open up the glass case covering God's presence. When the veil outside the Holy of Holies was torn, the presence of God became available to whomever would come and freely take. The glass case had been removed and the jewels of God's presence were made available. Just as the man's purchase made the jewelry store obsolete, the cross of Christ and the blood of Jesus made the temple unnecessary.

Sacrifices no longer needed to be given, for he was the one true sacrifice. Presence no longer needed to be sectioned off, for he had paid the price for the veil to be opened. The glass cases were destroyed, the price tags were taken off, and God's presence was no longer in the temple.

Now believers in Jesus are the new temples of God. The Almighty no longer dwells in stone and rock but in skin and bone. "Don't you know that you yourselves are God's temple and that God's Spirit dwells in your midst?" (1 Cor. 3:16 NIV). With the old temple, you had to come and be present with God. You had to make the trip, take the initiative, and experience God from a distance.

Now that we are the new temples of God, everything has changed. We don't have to go to God; God comes to us. There is no longer a pilgrimage but a mission. No longer a coming in but a sending out. No longer a distant presence but an intimate indwelling. Even Jesus said, "Come and see." But the Spirit within us says, "Go and tell." God broke all the rules of absence when he tore the veil and became present to us.

The God who was once absent and far off is now present and nearer than our skin. Like a diamond ring kept securely behind a case, God's presence was real but inaccessible to us. Jesus paid a high price for our entry into God's presence—his very life. This price bought for us the Holy Spirit, which is a new presence of God to us and represents so much more than it did by itself in the temple. Ephesians 2:19–22 tells us that we are no longer strangers or aliens to the family of God, but are growing into the holy temple of God as we are "being built together into a dwelling place for God by the Spirit." The Holy Spirit joins us to God.

I eventually did go to a jewelry store with more affordable

options and paid, what was to me, a high price. I took that expensive ring and asked my wife to marry me. That ring symbolized our joining together, our covenant, our commitment, and our lifelong presence with each other. The Holy Spirit, bought for us in Christ, does the same thing. The Holy Spirit is God's ring on our finger, guaranteeing what is to come.

New Connection

My wife and I got to go to France for our five-year anniversary. While we were in Paris we knew we had to go to the Louvre museum to see Leonardo da Vinci's famous *Mona Lisa*. On our way through the serpentine halls of the museum, we stopped and looked at a number of reputable paintings by Raphael, Dali, and Monet. We were able to walk right up to each of these masterpieces. We could have put our noses on the oil paint if we'd wanted to (and if we'd wanted to get kicked out).

But when we came to the room that housed the *Mona Lisa*, everything was different. There were swarms of people elbowing each other for a glimpse. A huge brass bar barrier gave the painting a wide berth of about six feet. On each side of the painting, attentive workers stood guard. And the painting itself was encased in glass. There was no getting close to this work of art.

I didn't get to connect with Leonardo da Vinci like I did with many other artists. I didn't get to spend time with his work, admire his brush strokes, and take in his mastery up close. But, when I think about it, I didn't get to connect with any of the artists as I would have liked. I didn't chat with Raphael or have tea with Dali. I didn't walk the halls of the Louvre with Monet or people watch with da Vinci. My connection with each of them was through a relic, an impression left by their skill.

It is this type of secondary connection that the majority of Israel had with God's presence before God sent his Spirit. They could only see God from afar, like I did with the *Mona Lisa*. There were walls, veils, guards, and crowds keeping them from enjoying God's presence in a more intimate way. But when the veil was torn and we became the new temples of the living God, the way we connect with the Almighty changed forever.

Not only does the Holy Spirit increase our capacity to experience and enjoy God, he also increases our ability to connect with God. We have to realize that the Holy Spirit is God's actual Spirit. Paul explained what a spirit is in 1 Corinthians 2:11: "For who knows a person's thoughts except the spirit of that person, which is in him? So also no one comprehends the thoughts of God except the Spirit of God."

The spirit is that central and eternal part of ourselves that is our core essence. It is our mind and its understanding, our heart and its feeling. And God has shared that part of himself with us. What a mystery! What a treasure!

Paul continued, "We have received not the spirit of the world, but the Spirit who is from God, that we might understand the things freely given us by God" (1 Cor. 2:12). The Holy Spirit connects us with the mind of God. In fact, Paul became so bold and pointed in his explanation of how the Holy Spirit connects us to God's mind that he said, "We have the mind of Christ" (v. 16). The same mind that allowed Jesus to live in perfect relationship with the Father dwells within us. We can connect with God as Jesus did through the Spirit.

What a reversal of absence. We were once shut out from God but now can know his Spirit. We were once cut off from God, but now he can live within us. We used to not know God at all, but now we have his very mind. The presence of God through his Spirit is an astounding mystery—a mystery we will never stop uncovering throughout our entire lives.

Absence in the Spirit

But you are probably wondering, as I have many times, *If the Holy Spirit dwells with me, how can God still feel absent? Shouldn't I feel complete if God is in me? Why does the Spirit feel insufficient? How can God feel absent when he is so present?* This is where the rubber of presence meets the road of absence. Because here, in our understanding of the Holy Spirit, we take our nearest experience of God and put it up against our most difficult questions of absence.

The Spirit and Sin

One of the times we feel far from God as Christians is when we sin. Like trying to casually talk to a friend you have wronged, our relationship with God just doesn't feel right until we have come to a resolution. You know your sins have been forgiven in Jesus, but there is a guilt barrier that still stands between you and the Father. The question we have to answer is whether this is a real experience of absence or just a misperception of guilt that we need to do away with.

There are two kinds of grief when it comes to sin. There is a worldly grief and a godly grief. Worldly grief is brought about by lies and legalism. The lies tell us that Jesus can't save us, that he doesn't care about us, that we are too evil for grace. These lies cause grief and contradict Scripture. Legalism tells us that we aren't doing enough, that we aren't as good as the other people in our church, and that we will never measure up to the right standard.

The legalism that causes grief contradicts the gospel. Worldly grief leads to loss and death. It is an unproductive grief that causes us to lose our faith and kill off our hope. Grief caused by lies and legalism draws us away from God instead of toward him. It draws us away from life and into death.

Godly grief is productive. Paul, in 2 Corinthians, was talking about a previous letter he sent (which we call 1 Corinthians), which must have caused a great deal of grief to the church in Corinth. His previous letter was full of rebukes and corrections that grieved the Corinthian church because they realized they were in much sin. "As it is, I rejoice, not because you were grieved, but because you were grieved into repenting. For you felt a godly grief, so that you suffered no loss through us. For godly grief produces a repentance that leads to salvation without regret, whereas worldly grief produces death" (7:9–10).

Godly grief causes repentance, while worldly grief causes condemnation. The Holy Spirit is the author of the former. Satan is the author of the latter. Repentance is turning away from our sin. The repentance caused by godly grief leads us not just to confess our sins but to kill our sins.

Jesus told the disciples that the Holy Spirit would bring them godly grief over their sins: "When he comes, he will prove the world to be in the wrong about sin and righteousness and judgment" (John 16:8 NIV). The Holy Spirit convicts us of sin. He brings godly grief that causes repentance.

This is an amazing twist on the presence of God when it comes to sin. Formerly, if God came near us, our sin would cause us to be destroyed. Now, when God comes near us in his Spirit, our sin is destroyed. God's presence now destroys sin instead of destroying us.

Therefore, if your guilt is making you feel far from God, you need to test where it is coming from. If it contradicts Scripture by telling you lies, or contradicts the gospel by condemning you with legalism, then it is the unproductive guilt of the world and must be done away with.

If, however, you are convicted of a sin, in accordance with Scripture, then you need to repent. You must stop sinning. After all, the Bible tells us that if we confess our sins we have fellowship with God (1 John 1:5–10). Repentance leads us into God's presence. Sin draws us into God's absence. Let the conviction of sin be a sign of the Spirit. The day you stop feeling grief over sin altogether may be the day you realize the Spirit is absent from you altogether.

Hear this well: Our repentance is directly linked to God's presence. Our holiness, that is, our conformity to the character of Christ has a direct effect on our ability to see God once we leave this world. Hebrews 12:14 puts this in clear and convicting language: "Strive for peace with everyone, and for the holiness without which no one will see the Lord." The Spirit convicts us of our sin for a very important purpose; because unless we turn from our sins, we will never be present with God in the way we most desire.

The Spirit and Distance

But how can we be absent from God when we sin and yet still have his Spirit? Are we on some kind of yo-yo string, moving away from God every time we sin and springing back to him every time we confess? Such a rocking journey of faith would surely make our souls seasick. How does this work?

As the Holy Spirit indwells Christians, we experience God in two main ways: faithfully and relationally. When we are saved through the blood of Jesus and given the gift of the Holy Spirit, our relationship with God's faithfulness has begun. His faithfulness to us is never ending and not dependent on the performance of individual believers. God is always faithfully present to those who are in Christ. But we are also relationally present with God. This is the part of our connection with God that has the qualities of a relationship. There is intimacy, interchange, movement, and fluidity. It is from God's relational presence that we occasionally feel absent.

Think of it like a marriage. Since I am classically trained at putting my foot in my mouth, I will set myself up as the hypothetical example. Imagine my wife and I are sitting on our couch in the living room. We are talking happily about our lives and how our days went. In my foolishness I completely ignore something particularly important my wife just said about her day so that I can jump to something I want to talk about that occurred at my work. She really wanted me to respond to this happening and celebrate with her regarding it.

Instead, I mow through her expectations and charge full speed ahead into my own prideful story. The whole mood of the living room changes as my wife's smile turns from an excited grin into an offended flat-line stare. She hasn't moved any farther away from me on the couch, but she feels infinitely farther from me than she did just one second ago. Why? Because I have breached the agreement of love and trust we have with each other.

She is still present with me but is far from me. This moment of stupidity hasn't made our marriage vows void, but it has put space between us. We are still faithfully present to each other in our marriage commitment, but we are distant from each other emotionally and relationally.

This is how relational distance works with God. When we sin against him and bolt on, unrepentant, through our lives, he may withdraw his relational presence from us. We feel it like the cold distance of a once-warm spouse. God does not do this because he is a vindictive meanie or an oversensitive grudge holder. He places absence between us so that, like the woman from Song of Solomon, we might pursue him and seek repentance. When we sin, the Holy Spirit doesn't leave the couch and storm out of the room. The faithful presence of God does not abandon us when we sin. We are still Christians, the Holy Spirit still dwells in us, but there is a relational gap.[1]

If you feel this gap between you and God, know that your salvation is not what is at risk. The intimacy of your relationship is suffering, not the state of your soul. But the gap is still dire, the absence still pressing. The Spirit may be using this feeling of relational absence to accomplish something significant in your life. You may be nursing a pet sin that you refuse to get rid of. The Holy Spirit has created absence between you and God so you will see that the pain of losing him is far worse than the pain of losing your sin.

You may have cut yourself off from the church. You figure you don't need the body of believers. But now the Spirit has started to feel far from you. Maybe he is using absence to show you that though there may be some difficulties in being part of the body of Christ, those difficulties are so worth it and so important to your relationship with Christ. The Holy Spirit uses relational absence to draw us closer to the Father, but at no time does he leave us, abandon us, or forsake us. His faithful presence is just that, faithful.

I want to take a moment to stop and offer a warning to you. The relational distance you feel from God is not just to lure you to his side, but to keep you safe from falling away from him forever. Sin puts relational distance between God and us throughout our lives. But a systemic heart of sin that continues throughout your life can be proof of a much more profound and eternal distance between you and God. Consider the stern words of Hebrews 3:12–14:

> See to it, brothers and sisters, that none of you has a sinful, unbelieving heart that turns away from the living God. But encourage one another daily, as long as it is called "Today," so that none of you may be hardened by sin's deceitfulness. We have

come to share in Christ, if indeed we hold our original conviction firmly to the very end. (NIV)

Without repentance, our hearts can grow hard and will turn
away from God. It will not be God who turns away from us, but
we who ultimately turn away from God. Sin is deceitful and will
trick you into thinking you are safe to continue living however you
want—safe to do all these "detestable things" as Jeremiah might
say. But remember that you will only find that you have come to
truly share in Christ if you hold firmly to the end your original conviction. If God feels far from you, repent and run to him. If there
is any relational distance between God and you due to sin, drop
everything that stands in your way and restore your relationship.

The Spirit and Dryness

Maybe you have read through this and thought, *But there's not
some big secret sin keeping me from God. I do attend church regularly
and read my Bible. Why does God still feel far? How can I have the
Holy Spirit and yet not feel him at all?* These are some of the questions that come out of those dark nights of the soul we journey
through. What we must realize is that the Spirit has not abandoned
us in these moments either. In fact, God's Spirit is doing mighty
work in us, even when our faith seems dry and our way seems dark.

The famous Twenty-third Psalm talks about a valley of darkness
where the shadow of death lies. You can imagine that this place is
pitch-dark. No light, no paths, no right way to be found. But in this
valley, vacant of light, God is there guiding us, even if we can't notice.
"Even though I walk through the darkest valley, I will fear no evil, for
you are with me; your rod and your staff, they comfort me" (v. 4 NIV).

Even when we are in darkness, God is with us. Even when we
cannot see the movement of our own feet, God is there guiding us.

He may use his rod and staff to harshly correct us, but it will be for our betterment. That is the role and the glory of the Holy Spirit. He is working inside of us, moving us to God.

The prophet Ezekiel talked about this kind of blind guidance as well. In Ezekiel 36:27, God was making a promise about the future of his people when he said, "I will put my Spirit in you and move you to follow my decrees" (NIV). The Holy Spirit comes on us and moves us to follow the will of God. Even when we don't feel like we are moving, or don't feel like moving at all, the Spirit causes us to move. The Holy Spirit moves us toward God even when we feel like we are at a standstill.

Think of it this way. The earth is always spinning, which means that you and I, even when we are standing completely still, are moving around at one thousand miles an hour. We are racing through our galaxy while sitting on the couch. No matter how lethargic or active we are, we are moving in relative motion—one thousand miles an hour every day. This is how the imperceptible movement of the Spirit can feel at times.[2]

You may feel stuck in a rut, like you haven't made one step toward God in years. You may feel like you are at a standstill in your faith, unable to move up the ladder of understanding or holiness. All the while God's Spirit is at work within you. In fact, his Spirit has never stopped. God is a ceaselessly moving force. No plan of his can be thwarted. No desire of his goes unfulfilled. When he put his Spirit in you, it was not in vain.

Don't get me wrong. The Spirit does bear fruit. Every true Christian should be producing a harvest of love, joy, peace, patience, kindness, goodness, faithfulness, gentleness, and self-control.[3] If the Spirit is within you, your life will take on these characteristics. But that doesn't mean that, like all natural harvests, our spirits can't experience a season of drought.

God has a plan for you because he has a plan for all creation. You may feel like you are in the belly of the fish, but God is moving you toward his purposes. You may think you aren't going anywhere, but God is moving you one thousand miles an hour toward himself.

The Spirit and the Future

There is still one more area of absence and the Holy Spirit that some of you may be thinking about. You may not be going through a relational separation caused by sin. And you may not feel like you are in a season of darkness. But you do feel like God is far off, even though you have the Spirit within you. This is because the Holy Spirit is pointing to the future.

It's like my granddad's example with the five dollars and the mutual fund. Since I have put my five dollars in, I'm guaranteed a future reward. I've put in my deposit and have secured my future inheritance. I have the mutual fund as a sign of presence, a promise of provision, and a form of security. But I don't yet have the full reward that will come when I cash it out.

The Holy Spirit is our mutual fund. The Bible says that God "set his seal of ownership on us, and put his Spirit in our hearts as a deposit, guaranteeing what is to come" (2 Cor. 1:22 NIV).

This idea is repeated in Ephesians 1:13–14: "When you believed, you were marked in him with a seal, the promised Holy Spirit, who is a deposit guaranteeing our inheritance" (NIV). The Holy Spirit is the present promise of a future reality. The Spirit is a guarantee that what is now absent will one day be present.

Even in God's nearest and most intimate presence, there is still a hint of absence. Even when God comes the closest to us, in his Spirit, he still points to the future. The future pledge of the Spirit does not negate the unflinching assurance of the promise, but it does show us that we will not be fully present with God until that promise comes true. God is absent in the way we most desire but present in the way we most require.

But, like my granddad's mutual fund account, we will be getting our reward with interest. The deposit of the Spirit is a down payment, a percentage, a small dose of what we will experience in heaven. The riches of God's presence will be had with compound returns. The pleasures of God's nearness will be experienced with exponentially multiplying dividends. The Spirit in us now guarantees God with us soon.

We have to remember that the Spirit that dwells in us is not the immediate presence of God the Father, nor is it some invisible version of Jesus the Son. The living God that is inside of the Christian is the distinct third member of the Trinity. So when we say, "God lives within me," we must be careful we don't assume that all our struggles with absence will melt away. The immediate presence of God is still absent from us. The relational, face-to-face intimacy we long for is still in the future.

The trash bags are still on the wall. However, now God's Spirit has come into the black-plastic room with us. Looking back on my time of worship in Red 2, I can now see that it was the Spirit awakening my senses to God. I wanted more of God because he had shown me the pleasure of his Spirit. The Holy Spirit awakens our senses to the glory of God. The nearness between the Spirit and us enlightens our eyes to the distance between God and us.

FOURTEEN

SOONER THAN WE DESERVE, BUT NOT AS SOON AS WE DESIRE

What will eternal presence

and absence be like?

I see him, but not now;
I behold him, but not near.
—NUMBERS 24:17

Absence longs to be reconciled to presence. We want to join back up with what we once had. Whether it's the high school football star who wishes he could relive the glory days, or the child who lost her dog and aches to find him, when something treasured becomes absent, we long for it to be present again. One of the most significant moments of reconciliation I have ever experienced was with my dad, which occurred several years after my parents got divorced.

When my dad left, I placed all the blame on him. From the inside of our now emptier home, I watched my mom wrestle with the pain of abandonment, the confusion of loneliness, and the struggles of being a single mom. She fought the divorce. Every night for months on end, she would put a candle in the front window of our home, signifying that she was still committed to the marriage. She longed for what she had to be restored. Every time that candle was lit, a new fire burned in my soul too.

I harbored shipping containers full of bitterness and resentment toward my father. One night I decided I would confront him honestly about my anger and disappointment. We went to a nice meal at one of my favorite restaurants, just the two of us. I was fourteen at the time. I looked at him from across the table and said, "I have lost all respect for you." The space that had grown between us since the divorce now had a big neon sign pointing it out. My dad and I were absent from each other.

He was not physically absent. He consistently picked me up at school once a week for lunch. He invited me over to his apartment to stay the night and play on his new Xbox. We were still near each other physically, but we were hundreds of miles and years apart relationally.

The distance remained for years. These were formative years. I was far from my dad while he taught me to drive my stick shift '93 Ford Ranger. I was far from my dad when I fell in love with the woman who is now my wife. I was far from my dad when I went to my senior prom. I was far from my dad when I moved into my college dorm. My dad and I saw each other regularly, but the relational distance was always there, glowing dimly beneath the sign I had erected all those years before.

But one night during my sophomore year of college, my dad

and I stumbled into some deep conversation territory while sitting around his house late at night. As the single digits of the morning began to creep up on the clock, my courage and resolution grew within me. I asked my dad if he would tell me the whole story of what happened between my mom and him over the years. He obliged.

It took hours to hear all the backstory and side roads of my dad's life in college before he met my mom, the first tiny apartment they shared in a bad part of town, and how the relational chasm of absence grew between them over the years. It was hard to hear, but it was worth it.

When he finally got to the end of the story, an unexpected sentiment came tumbling out of my dad's mouth. He apologized. But not only that, he repented to me. He told me that if there was any way he could take it back, he would. He was so sorry for how he'd hurt me. As tears spilled out of my strong father's eyes, the relational gap began to close between us. Week by week, conversation by conversation, we have been reconstructing our relationship. He is now a dear friend, a wise counselor, and a reliable helper throughout my life.

My dad and I were absent from each other relationally, but reconciliation brought us back together.

This is a shadow of the reconciliation we look forward to with our Father God. As we have seen throughout this book, God is absent from us in a multiplicity of different ways. He is far from us physically and, at times, he is far from us relationally. But God, through Scripture, tells us that our story will end in reconciliation. Jesus will return, heaven and earth will be remade, and God will make his dwelling with us. Like my dad's story, once told, brought us back together, the story of God, once finished, will bring presence like a flood into our dry world of absence.

The End of the Story

When we think about the second coming of Jesus and the end of the Bible, many of our minds go to the book of Revelation. Don't worry, we will not be picking apart that difficult book. This isn't the Left Behind series, nor is it a commentary on what the beast with ten horns and seven heads represents. There are plenty of verses in Scripture that clearly and beautifully describe what will happen when God's story reaches its climax. We are simply going to look at the clear pictures of presence that are promised to us.

All Christians look forward to the day when Jesus will return.[1] At the second coming of his presence, many things we look forward to will happen. First of all, Jesus will enter our world for the second time. "The Lord himself will come down from heaven, with a loud command, with the voice of the archangel and with the trumpet call of God" (1 Thess. 4:16 NIV). This is the moment we have all been waiting for: when Jesus himself will return to us in his truest form.

The one who first entered the world to the sound of livestock and in the company of a stable will return to the sound of a heavenly trumpet and in the company of angels. He who first entered the world at its lowest point will return to it from its highest. The one who rode into Jerusalem on the back of a donkey will ride into the world upon the billows of clouds. The suffering servant will return as the conquering king.

Like the voice that booms over the loudspeakers in a basketball arena as each player is announced before they take the court, the whole world will know who is about to enter the stadium of this world. As his name is announced and the trumpet is sounded, "the dead in Christ will rise first" (1 Thess. 4:16).

Imagine this sight: Cemeteries coming alive, oceans giving up their ashes, unmarked graves finally putting names on the unknown who slept inside. This will not be some zombie horror show. The new lives coming out of the old graves will not be the living dead. There will be nothing grotesque or macabre about the raising of the dead. Those who died trusting in Jesus will be raised just as he was: with a new resurrected body.

At the sound of the trumpet, the world's population will be filled with glorified physical bodies. The resurrected body will not be a mummy, nor will it be an angel. We will look like Jesus did when he was raised from the tomb.[2] People could walk with him down a road, eat with him by the sea, and touch the scars on his flesh. We will have our bodies, but they will be new, perfect, complete, and whole, as they never were before.

Think of resurrection not like a horror film but rather like a nature documentary. We are not talking about corpses rising from the grave but butterflies emerging from their chrysalis. The resurrection is caterpillar legs turning into monarch wings. The resurrection is a beautiful flower growing out of the ground from the tiny seed that went into it. What was planted in the ground is only a shadow of what will be raised from it. Our bodies are the seeds. Glory is the crop.[3]

Those who are alive will also put on their new resurrected bodies at the second coming of Jesus. "We will not all sleep, but we will all be changed—in a flash, in the twinkling of an eye, at the last trumpet. For the trumpet will sound, the dead will be raised imperishable, and we will be changed. For the perishable must clothe itself with the imperishable, and the mortal with immortality" (1 Cor. 15:51–53 NIV).

Once the dead in Christ put on their resurrected bodies and join Jesus in the sky, those "who are still alive and are left will be caught up together with them in the clouds to meet the Lord in the air. And so we will be with the Lord forever" (1 Thess. 4:17 NIV). All

Christians will meet Christ in the air. We will meet his presence in the clouds and dwell with him forever.

Don't worry, we will not be staying in the clouds. The images of angels sitting on fluffy white cumulus wisps and plucking their harps has done more harm than good for the general view of what heaven will be like. We will not stay in the sky, but we will return to a newly made earth. Like a busboy picks up all condiment holders and table-tent signs before wiping the table clean, Jesus will lift us out of the world to reset the table. And as surely as the set pieces will return to any chain restaurant table once it is all shiny and new, so will we return to a new earth wiped clean of all the filth left behind by its former patrons.

The image of meeting Jesus in the clouds would have actually been a very familiar idea for the Bible's original audience. Biblical scholar Anthony Hoekema explained that when a visiting ruler came to a city in Bible times, the citizens would go out to meet him as he entered the gates. But they didn't hang out at the gates. The citizens would walk the ruler, in a parade of honor and celebration, back into their city for him to conduct his business.

We, too, will meet Jesus as our visiting ruler and will celebrate in his train as we make our way back onto our new earth. After meeting Jesus in the air, the Lord will not "reverse his direction and go back to heaven."[4] We will return to our newly created earth in the train of our reigning king Jesus. But unlike a visiting ruler, Jesus is not just coming back for a brief stay. He is coming back to move in with us.

A New Home with God

What is the new earth? The apostle John gave us a vision of this coming future moment in Revelation 21:1–2: "Then I saw 'a new heaven and a new earth,' for the first heaven and the first earth had passed away, and there was no longer any sea. I saw the Holy City, the new Jerusalem, coming down out of heaven from God, prepared as a bride beautifully dressed for her husband" (NIV).

When Jesus returns, he will not only bring himself but a new creation. "I am making everything new!" Jesus said (Rev. 21:5 NIV). We will live neither in the uncharted floating cloud city of a fictionalized heaven nor back in the broken remains of the fallen world in which we now reside. Neither our fake views of heaven nor our current view of the world will be our future home.

A perfected earth will be the residence of our perfected bodies. Just as our flesh will be changed into a glorious, resurrected form, so the earth will take on a newly born image and character. The earth isn't God's failed science project that will be tossed out in the garbage bin after the fair is over. Earth is part of God's good design. Just like us, God made the earth with a purpose in mind—to be the home we would live in together.

In God's ultimate moment of presence, he will abandon heaven and come to earth.[5] The first heaven, God's home, will pass away so that he can come build a new home with us. God will leave his perfect world to come renovate ours. He will demolish his old place to come construct a new one for us.

The old heaven and the old earth represent two different dwelling places. Now God lives in heaven and we live on earth. But when God destroys the first heaven and earth, he will be showing us that these boundaries, borders, and sections are not suitable for the kind of presence God wants to share with us. God will do away with two so he can create one. The new heaven and new earth will be the one house God and man will share for eternity. When Jesus returns, God will move in.[6]

God's presence in the new earth won't be like his presence in the temple. In fact, it will be the exact opposite. Revelation 21:22 speaks about how different God's presence in the new earth will be from his presence in the old temple in these words: "And I saw no temple in the city, for its temple is the Lord God the Almighty and the Lamb." God won't *dwell* in a temple. God will *be* the temple. There is no more need for containment, mediation, rules, or boundaries. God removes all of them when his presence becomes the way we interact with his presence.

The trumpet won't be the only sound coming from the clouds on that day. There will also be a wonderful proclamation made: "I heard a loud voice from the throne saying, 'Look! God's dwelling place is now among the people, and he will dwell with them. They will be his people, and God himself will be with them and be their God'" (Rev. 21:3 NIV).

There will no longer be absence between our home and God's home. We won't live in separate neighborhoods. We won't work in different cities. We will ditch our long-distance relationship, get married, and move in together. This is the moment all creation is longing for. We long for our new bodies, and the earth itself longs for its own recreation. Romans 8:22–23 says it beautifully:

> For we know that the whole creation has been groaning together in the pains of childbirth until now. And not only the creation, but we ourselves, who have the firstfruits of the Spirit, groan inwardly as we wait eagerly for adoption as sons, the redemption of our bodies.

Immanuel will return and God will be with us. The presence we always longed for will be with us in a way we never could have imagined. The black trash bags of our world will be burned up faster than a magician's flash paper, and God will enter our rooms of absence. His presence will comfort us, heal us, and complete us. He will wipe away every tear from our eyes. There will no longer be death, pain, crying, or mourning. Medicine will be a memory. Time will be a tale. Hospitals will seem like they were no more than a hallucination. Death will seem like it was nothing more than a door.

The presence of God will blot out even the faintest aroma of absence. The bushes we jumped into to hide, we will be called out of. The cleft of the rock in which we hid will split open so we may stand in God's presence. The once-elusive presence that made brief touches only to slip through our fingers will stand resolute and unmoving before us forever. The lover that jiggled the handle will rip the door off its hinges.

The presence of God that once seemed sequestered to church experiences and fled from our manipulation will surround us as church walls never did and will move us in ways we never could move God. The tears that streamed from our faces as we scraped our sores with pottery will be wiped away with all our discomforts and diseases. The belly of darkness we sat in for so long will spew us out onto the shores of glory.

All that was absent will now be present. All that was present will now be manifest. All that was gone will now be here. All that was hidden will now be seen. Heaven will be where we live with God on the new earth. Heaven will be the place where the promise of Deuteronomy 33:27 finally comes true: "The eternal God is your dwelling place."

Absence in the Second Coming

It would be a lot easier if the book ended here. But that would not be honest to the picture of all the second coming of Jesus will accomplish. Jesus' return will bring the most profound moment of presence, but it will also bring the most devastating mode of absence. The presence of heaven is not the only new reality this day will create. The day Jesus returns will also bring the absence of hell.

Many of the Bible verses that proclaimed the good news we read about above came from one of Paul's letters, 1 Thessalonians. He used beautiful language to talk about the day of Christ's return as a day of presence. Paul described us meeting Jesus in the air and living with him forever. This same author wrote another letter to the same church concerning the same day. The second letter Paul wrote to them is called 2 Thessalonians. In the first few lines of that letter, Paul talked about the second coming of Jesus again. But this time, Paul did not use beautiful language to talk about presence; he used painful language to talk about absence.

> God is just: He will pay back trouble to those who trouble you and give relief to you who are troubled, and to us as well. This will happen when the Lord Jesus is revealed from heaven in blazing fire with his powerful angels. He will punish those who do not know God and do not obey the gospel of our Lord Jesus. *They will be . . . shut out from the presence of the Lord* and from the glory of his might. (1:6–9 NIV, emphasis mine)

For many people, the day of the Lord's presence will be the beginning of his absence. If heaven is where God is, hell is where God is not. Heaven is where the mercy of God is experienced forever. Hell is where the justice of God is experienced forever. Everything that is present in heaven will be absent in hell.

In heaven, God will wipe away every tear from our eyes. In hell, there will be weeping and gnashing of teeth. Hell is being separated from every good thing, because hell is being separated from God, the only good thing. In heaven, God will be present in the way we most desire (his glory) but absent in the way we most require (his wrath). In hell, the opposite is just as true.

We have no way of understanding what this absence will be like. A secluded man living alone in an apartment may feel absent from the rest of the world. It is hard for him to see himself as part of society. He has no friends, no one to connect with, no groups to be a part of, and no place where he belongs other than his small apartment. There is a great deal of absence in this man's life.

However, if this man was moved into solitary confinement, out in the middle of nowhere, he would experience a level of absence like never before. He could not leave his box. He could not people watch. He could not listen to the hum of cars driving by, conversations being had, or life being lived. Absence can get exponentially worse.

We do not live in God's complete absence right now. He is generally present with us. His abiding presence sustains the world and keeps it inside his will. Even though God can feel quite absent in this world, hell will be an absence like nothing we've ever experienced. Absence may feel like being alone in an apartment, but hell will be complete separation.

You may feel far from God now, but hell will take distance out of the equation. Hell is not being one million miles away from the goodness of God. Hell is being in a world without the goodness of God. When Jesus returns, he will not say, "You go to your corner of eternity and we will go to ours." Hell is complete separation. Hell is absolute absence.

You may have made it this far in the book and find yourself thinking, *I don't want to be absent from God forever. I want to be found in his presence.* If that is you, it is imperative that I take a moment and explain how to escape eternal absence. You have already read the story of the gospel—how Jesus endured absence so we could be in God's presence. God not only became flesh to take on the absence we deserved but the pain and the punishment we deserved too.

We are all sinners. Every single person in the world has broken God's eternal law and must be held accountable for breaking that law.[7] The only punishment suitable for an eternal soul that has broken the eternal law of the only eternal God is eternal punishment. That eternal punishment is separation from all the goodness of God for all the fullness of eternity.

The reason God must punish us in this way is because he is holy and just. Many of us know that God is love, but he is more than that. God is not just love. He is also holy. He has a holy love. Because he is holy, he must hold sinners responsible for their sin. But because he is love, he does not want to see his creation punished. God has a holy love, and both parts work in concert with one another. They are not contradictory. God refuses to act in love at the expense of his holiness or in holiness at the expense of his love.[8]

So God satisfied his holy love by dying the death and so bearing the judgment we deserved. As the late British theologian John Stott put it, he both "exacted" and "accepted" the penalty of human sin. Romans 3:26 explains it this way: "It was to show his righteousness at the present time, so that he might be just and the justifier of the one who has faith in Jesus."

In his holiness he was just, by pouring out his wrath. In his love he was the justifier, by being the one his wrath was poured out upon. He is just because he punished. He is justifier because he punished himself. He is holy because punishment was carried out. He is love because it was carried out upon himself.

The one who made the law took on its punishments. The one who holds men responsible became responsible himself. God is the only one who could do this. God became flesh in the person of Jesus Christ so that he could bear his own punishment. This is the gospel story, and it is the only way that we can be in God's presence instead of his absence forever.

If you have never heard this story, or never believed that it was true until now, I invite you to respond right now wherever you are reading this book. How you are to respond is simple. Your response is in the Bible verse from Romans we just read. God the just will be your justifier if you have faith in Jesus. The book of Romans also says, "If you declare with your mouth, 'Jesus is Lord,' and believe in your heart that God raised him from the dead, you will be saved" (10:9 NIV).

So no matter where you are, if you believe that Jesus took on the punishment that you deserved and was raised from the dead, I invite you to say to God, "Jesus is Lord." There is nothing we can do to earn the salvation and presence of God, and this is what he requires of us. So if you have said this prayer, I invite you to find a local church in your area and tell them that you have put your faith in Jesus.

The Good News of Absence

We must remember that since God is good, even in his use of hell there is good news to be told. But many people have a mixed-up view of what hell will be. Though we don't have a wealth of information in the Bible to go on, I am confident that hell will look as different from our imagined images of pitchforks and fire chambers as heaven will from our perceived pictures of harps and clouds.

Hell is not some cartoon pit where a pitchfork-wielding devil hooks his prisoners up to different torture devices. Satan is not the master of hell; God is. Satan is not the distributer of punishment; God is. Satan is numbered in the population of those being punished in hell. The Devil is not the warden of hell; he is among its first inmates.

Along with a few other characters from the book of Revelation, Satan, death, and Hades—which is another word for the grave—are all sent to eternal punishment when Jesus returns. Revelation 20 makes this clear: "The devil, who deceived them, was thrown into the lake of burning sulfur, where the beast and the false prophet had been thrown. They will be tormented day and night for ever and ever. . . . Then death and Hades were thrown into the lake of fire" (vv. 10, 14 NIV).

Not only Satan, but death and the grave are sent to hell as well. When the living Jesus returns, death dies. When heaven comes, the grave goes to hell. When the Lord moves to earth, Satan is moved to Hades. What an amazing picture. What an amazing truth.

Satan, evil, death, pain, funerals, hospitals, guns, prisons, weeping, and good-byes will all be absent in heaven. Everything God is not will be sent away. Without hell there cannot be heaven. Without absence there cannot be presence. What keeps us from enjoying God as we most desire must be sent away in the manner we most require.

Sooner Than We Deserve, but Not As Soon As We Desire

Jesus is coming back. Presence is on its way. We deserve absence. He is bringing presence. God's visible and actual presence will be consummated fully in the return of Jesus. The person of Jesus is the form of presence we most long to see. The body that was raised from the tomb is the face-to-face meeting with God we have longed for all our lives. Jesus is God's presence made perfect.

The presence of God walking in the garden that Adam and Eve lost in the fall, will return to us. This presence is none other than Jesus himself. The second person in the Trinity, who came to be known to us as Jesus, was the one who walked the garden in the cool of the day. He is returning to walk with us. As one of the early church fathers Tertullian put it:

> For [Jesus] always descended to hold converse with men, from Adam even to the patriarchs and prophets, in visions, in dreams, in mirrors, in dark sentences, always preparing his way from the beginning: neither was it possible, that God who conversed with men upon earth, could be any other than the Word which was to be made flesh.[9]

The presence of God that all humanity has desired is returning in the person of Jesus. This presence is coming sooner than we deserve, because even if we lived a hundred lifetimes, we would never deserve it. But presence does not come as soon as we desire. We are stuck in the black trash-bag room of this world. We want God's presence now. We want to take what we could only imagine and see it for what it truly is, but we cannot step into this presence yet. Therefore, as Clooney succinctly stated, God comes "sooner than we deserve but not as soon as we desire."[10]

Absence is our address on this earth, even while we are waiting for God to move into the neighborhood. Our sinful flesh separates us from God, as it did Adam and Eve in the garden. We are forced to stand in the cleft of the rock while begging God for more, like Moses. God's presence may feel elusive, like it was to Abraham, but we can trust that the people group God began with Isaac will be completed out of every tribe and every nation.

It may feel like you have searched for God and found him not, but he is jiggling the handle of your heart and one day he will be found standing on the other side. While in this state of absence, we must learn to hold fast to humble confidence without slipping into proud entitlement. For now, we suffer pain on this earth, though we know God is preparing us for presence like Job. We may go through dark nights of the soul within the belly of the fish, but we know that, like Jonah, God is bringing us to himself.

The presence of God was earned for us through the blood of Christ. Nothing else in this world can bring us to God except the death, burial, and resurrection of Jesus. Only his sacrifice was rich enough to pay the high cost of entry into the Holy of Holies for us all. While we are on this earth, we have the Spirit as a deposit guaranteeing what is to come. And what is to come is a glorious eternity of presence, a wonderful undoing of absence, and an unfathomable reconciliation between God and man.

For now we wait. We wait for God to return sooner than we deserve but not as soon as we desire.

ACKNOWLEDGMENTS

With sickening incredulity I have often heard the perennial platitude, "I was truly humbled through this process" when authors refer to their works. My admittedly sinful presumption was to read false humility and true pride into lines such as these. Yet, here I find myself at the end of penning my first book and I have no other words to contribute other than this cliché toward which I held such animosity.

I have been truly humbled through this process. In fact, I have been humiliated by this process; humiliated by my ignorant mind and my imprecise language. I have been humiliated by the grand thinkers who have gone before me to lay such a wide and solid foundation upon which I have erected this rickety hut of a thought. I have been humiliated by the original ideas I brought to the formation of this book that God's Word would not allow. I am humiliated at the persistency with which I tried to fit the square peg of my hypothesis into the round hole of God's truth. Chiefly, I am humiliated by the condescension of the Son of God as man Jesus. I have been humiliated in the best of ways. I have met Christ anew in writing these pages and seen him as gloriously near though infinitely far. Truly, I have been humbled.

One of the most steady and joyful humiliations of this process was making myself vulnerable to the many people without which I could not have accomplished this work.

Taylor Walling has been an endless treasure of a friend and a vast resource for clear communication and balanced thinking. His "book doctoring" work alongside me (whether in Cincinnati, Dallas, or Oklahoma City) has reaped countless benefits to the words in this volume. I am lovingly indebted to him for the clarity of this book as should the reader be.

J. J. Seid, my mentor and friend, suffered long with me through my season of feeling far from God. His guidance and steadfast love for Jesus was instrumental in drawing me out of absence and into presence.

My pastor, Sam Storms, has contributed greatly to my pursuit of the face of God and my commitment to the gospel of Jesus Christ. The consistency with which I was able to find Jesus in absence and present him to the reader owes a debt of gratitude to Sam.

This book would not exist without Lisa Jackson who reached out to me and shepherded this book from concept to completion. She has been far more than a literary agent for me in this process, as a friend, champion, and rock.

Dudley Chancey is a man to whom I owe so many of the opportunities God has brought my way. Through Dudley, the Lord has given me the great pleasure of growing as a communicator and lover of the truth of God.

Perhaps no group was more fundamental to the development of this book or the sustaining of my own soul and sanity than my discipleship group: Brady Easter, Seth Stewart, and Kelcy White. Thank you all for fighting for truth in my book and against sin in my life.

I must also acknowledge Drew Chancey, a dear friend and constant encouragement. Thank you for your insights and for constantly reminding me how excited you have been to read this book. Knowing that kept me going.

Dave Boden, my British-best-friend and nearest namesake, has been a source of intercession and joy throughout this process. Thank you for believing in me and building into me as a friend and guide.

My wife, Meagan, was a ceaseless advocate for this work. Thank you Meagan for sacrificing our time for my study, writing, and proofreading. I could not have done this without you at my side.

Finally, I would like to thank Mother Teresa, St. John of the Cross, and John Frame (a unique clash of characters) who have ventured to faithfully and honestly discuss God's absence in their own panoply of unique and helpful ways. I am indebted to your lives and works.

NOTES

Chapter 1: Hummers and Birthstones

1. Samuel Rutherford, *The Loveliness of Christ* (Edinburgh: Banner of Truth Trust, 2015), 3.
2. C. S. Lewis, *Mere Christianity* (San Francisco, CA: HarperCollins, 2001), 136–37.

Chapter 2: Trash Bag Covered Walls

1. Exodus 25:8, 33:18; Psalm 16:11, 27:4, 130:5–6, 132; Romans 8:19–23; Revelation 21:1–11.
2. Genesis 3:8, 17:7–8; Exodus 6:7; Leviticus 26:12; Jeremiah 30:22, 31:33, 32:38; Ezekiel 11:20, 36:28, 37:27; Zechariah 2:10–11, 8:8; Hosea 2:23; 2 Corinthians 6:16; Hebrews 8:10; Revelation 21:3.
3. John 1:1, 14; Colossians 2:9; Philippians 2:5–11; Hebrews 1:8.
4. David Murray, *Jesus on Every Page: 10 Simple Ways to Seek and Find Christ in the Old Testament* (Nashville, TN: Thomas Nelson, 2013), 77.
5. For a more full treatment of how sin affected the relationship between man and God, see: Christopher W. Morgan and Robert A. Peterson, *Fallen: A Theology of Sin* (Wheaton, IL: Crossway, 2013), 131–62.
6. Numbers 17:12–13; Isaiah 59:2; Habakkuk 1:13; Romans 3:23; 2 Thessalonians 1:9.
7. Romans 3:25–26.

8. J. R. R. Tolkien, *The Fellowship of the Ring: The Lord of the Rings Part One* (New York, NY: Mariner Books, 2012), 369.

9. In fact, God promises the sacrifice of Jesus before removing Adam and Eve from Eden. Genesis 3:15 promises that one of Eve's offspring will crush Satan and all he caused. This is the earliest and first promise of Jesus we find in our Bibles.

10. Galatians 3:27–29.

11. 1 Corinthians 15:50; 1 John 3:2, 4:12.

Chapter 3: God: Absent and Everywhere

1. J. Ryan Lister, *The Presence of God: Its Place in the Storyline of Scripture and the Story of Our Lives* (Wheaton, IL: Crossway, 2014), 33. For a great resource on God's presence, please refer to Lister's book.

2. Deuteronomy 4:37.

3. God himself explains the difference between his general and relational presence when forming his unique relationship with Israel after he rescues them from Egypt. "You shall be my treasured possession among all peoples, for all the earth is mine" (Ex. 19:5b). The whole earth belongs to God, and he is generally present in it, but he chose a special group of people for his relational kind of presence. He would be more present and present in a different way with Israel than he would be with the rest of the world. God is present in the world, but not relationally present with everyone in it. God is in the café, but if you are not in Christ, he will not be at your table. So you can see, there are different modes or levels of presence. God can be generally present to the world and relationally present with Christians. Beyond that, he can be relationally present with Christians, but still visually and actually absent from them.

Chapter 4: The Moses Principle: More Wants More

1. As Samuel Terrien has said, the thick cloud "is the symbol both of divine presence and of divine hiddenness" (*The Elusive Presence*, 128). Therefore, even in this remarkable moment of presence, God is still wrapped in absence.

2. Exodus 19:12–13, 21–25.

3. There are moments in the Old Testament, even in Exodus, where a human is said to speak with God face-to-face. But these ideas are not in contradiction. As Samuel Terrien has written, "Biblical Hebrew did not apparently possess an abstract word meaning 'presence.' The expression 'the face of Yahweh' or 'the face of Elohim' was sometimes specifically used to designate the innermost being of God, inaccessible even to a man like Moses, but panîm, 'face,' was ordinarily used metaphorically in composite prepositions to designate a sense of immediate proximity" (*The Elusive Presence*, 65). In fact, the idea of speaking to God face-to-face was less of a a physical reality and more of an idiom indicating intimacy (*The Elusive Presence*).

4. Exodus 19:16–20.

5. Deuteronomy 4:12.

6. Timothy Keller, *Counterfeit Gods* (New York, NY: Riverhead Books, 2009), xii–xiii.

7. Exodus 32:20.

8. 2 Corinthians 3:7, 9.

9. Matthew 5:14.

Chapter 5: The Far-Off Promises of an Elusive God

1. For more information about the Seed Company, visit www.theseed company.org.

2. "Monty Python and the Holy Grail quotes," Movie Quote DB, http://www.moviequotedb.com/movies/monty-python-and-the-holy -grail/quote_15697.html.

3. Titus 2:11–13, quoted at the beginning of this chapter, shows us that the grace of God has appeared, but we are still waiting. Jesus has come, but we are still waiting for him. We are like the priestly order who did not receive an inheritance in the promised land but were told that their portion was God himself (Num. 18:20). See also 1 Peter 2:11.

4. Genesis 12:1–3, 16:1.

5. Genesis 16:1–2.

6. Genesis 17:4–8.

7. Abraham was seventy-five years old when he left Haran after being

called by God (Gen. 12:5). Abraham was eighty-six years old when Ishmael was born (Gen. 16:16), making it roughly ten years since he left Haran that he laid with Hagar and eleven years since when Ishmael was born. Finally, Abraham was one hundred years old when Isaac was born (Gen. 21:5), making it twenty-five years since God's promise.

8. John 1:46.

Chapter 6: Sick with Love

1. There are seemingly innumerable interpretations of Song of Solomon, who its characters represented, and what exactly was happening within each part of the book. I am taking what I find to be the most straightforward and literal interpretation of the text. Regardless of your interpretation of Song of Solomon, I hope you can find truth in my treatment of it.

2. Song of Solomon 1:15–16.

3. Song of Solomon 2:4.

4. Song of Solomon 5:2–8.

5. Francis X. Clooney, S.J., *His Hiding Place Is Darkness: A Hindu-Catholic Theopoetics of Divine Absence* (Stanford, CA: Stanford University Press, 2013), 6, 33.

6. Wayne Grudem, *Systematic Theology: An Introduction to Biblical Doctrine* (Grand Rapids, MI: Zondervan, 2000), 150–52.

7. Clooney, *His Hiding Place Is Darkness*, 120.

8. For a great explanation of the necessity for God to reveal himself to us, see: Grudem, *Systematic Theology*, 149.

9. James 4:8 promises us that if we draw near to God, he will draw near to us. We should fully lean on this promise but take into account the fiction of duration and direction. It has always been God who has first drawn near to us (Rom. 5:8), and we have an eternity of drawing near to him ahead of us. So though God is near, he may still feel far because of the sheer distance between us. Moving one mile closer to a destination one thousand miles away doesn't seem like much of an achievement. But it is. And such a move toward God is a mighty achievement as well.

10. Clooney, *His Hiding Place Is Darkness*, 69.
11. Ibid., 121.
12. Deuteronomy 4:29.

Chapter 7: When God Stops Coming to Church

1. Leviticus 16; Hebrews 9:7.
2. Israel should have been used to this idea of God removing his presence from them when their lives were out of sync with his will since they had experienced it before in their conquest of the promised land (see Deut. 1:42).
3. T. Desmond Alexander, while talking about God's presence leaving the temple in the book of Ezekiel, says, "The idolatry, bloodshed and injustice of the people has forced God to leave the temple and the city." These are the exact same sins that Jeremiah raised against the people in Jeremiah 7. Therefore, it is not hard to see that if God was not already driven out by the people's injustice, he would soon be on his way. *From Eden to the New Jerusalem: An Introduction to Biblical Theology* (Grand Rapids, MI: Kregel, 2009), 56. See also, Ezekiel 8:3–16.
4. It is difficult to pinpoint exactly when God's presence left the temple. The language of Jeremiah makes it sound like God's presence was already gone, if not teetering on the fence. We do know, however, that God's presence did finally leave the temple because it is recorded in Ezekiel 8–11. For a detailed explanation of God's absence in the temple, see: John F. Kutsko, *Between Heaven and Earth: Divine Presence and Absence in the Book of Ezekiel* (Winona Lake, IN: Eisenbrauns, 2000), 151–52.
5. Samuel Terrien, *The Elusive Presence* (Eugene, OR: Wipf & Stock, 2000), 255.
6. Deuteronomy 14:24–26.
7. N. T. Wright, *Jesus and the Victory of God* (Minneapolis, MN: Fortress Press, 1996), 423.
8. David Murray, *Jesus on Every Page* (Nashville, TN: Thomas Nelson, 2013), 96, emphasis in original.
9. John 14:21.

10. T. Desmond Alexander, *From Eden to the New Jerusalem*, 69.

11. See Ephesians 2:19–22.

Chapter 8: Where Two or Three Are Gathered

1. David Bowden, "How Can We but Celebrate (Celebration)" *12*, 2012.

2. Deuteronomy 17:6, 19:15.

3. John Piper, *Desiring God* (Colorado Springs, CO: Multnomah, 2001), 43.

4. Ibid., 47.

5. Ibid., 48, emphasis in original.

6. Ibid., 50.

7. 1 Corinthians 14:15.

8. Isaiah 29:13; Matthew 15:8.

9. John Calvin, *Commentaries on the Epistle to the Hebrews*, trans. John Owen (Grand Rapids, MI: Wm. B. Eerdmans, 1949), on 2:12.

10. Alexander explains that though the church is the new temple in which God's presence dwells, the church is not the full and final end of God's presence. "Although the church plays an important role in both modeling and partially realizing God's creation blueprint for the earth," that is that God's presence would fill all of creation fully, "it too, like the Jerusalem temple, has limitations. For the ultimate realization of God's purposes for the world we must look to the New Jerusalem of Revelation 21–22." *From Eden to the New Jerusalem*, 60–61.

11. John Piper, *Desiring God*, 18.

12. Zephaniah 3:17. For more on God rejoicing over us, see: Sam Storms, *The Singing God: Feel the Passion God Has for You . . . Just the Way You Are* (Lake Mary, FL: Passio, 2013).

Chapter 9: Presence in Suffering

1. Acts 14:22.

2. "It Is Well with My Soul," Wikipedia, last modified April 1, 2016, https://en.wikipedia.org/wiki/It_Is_Well_with_My_Soul.

3. Job 1:14–19.

4. For a more full treatment of suffering in Job, see D. A. Carson, *How Long, O Lord? Reflections on Suffering and Evil* (Grand Rapids, MI: Baker Academic, 2006), 135–57.

5. Elie Wiesel, *Night* (New York, NY: Hill and Wang, 2012), 65.

6. Job 38:1.

7. D. A. Carson, *How Long, O Lord?*; John Piper and Justin Taylor, *Suffering and the Sovereignty of God*; C. S. Lewis, *The Problem of Pain;* Timothy Keller, *Walking with God through Pain and Suffering.*

8. C. S. Lewis, *The Weight of Glory: And Other Addresses* (New York, NY: HarperCollins, 2001), 37.

Chapter 10: That Safe Darkness

1. Mother Teresa, *Come Be My Light*, ed. Brian Kolodiejchuk (New York, NY: Image, 2007), 187.

2. Ibid., 180.

3. Ibid., 164.

4. Jonah 1:1.

5. Nahum 3:1 NIV.

6. Psalm 139:7–9.

7. Francis Thompson, *The Hound of Heaven and Other Poems* (Wellesley, MA: Branden Books, 2000), 11. The poem is public domain in the USA.

8. Jonah 1:12.

9. E. Allison Peers, *Dark Night of the Soul: A Masterpiece in the Literature of Mysticism* (New York, NY: Doubleday, 2005), 30.

10. Ibid., 108.

11. Psalm 39:13.

12. J. C. Ryle, *Holiness* (CreateSpace, 2013), 120.

13. David Scott, *A Revolution of Love: The Meaning of Mother Teresa* (Chicago, IL: Loyola Press, 2001), 154.

14. Gerald G. May, M.D., *The Dark Night of the Soul: A Psychiatrist Explores the Connection Between Darkness and Spiritual Growth* (New York, NY: HarperCollins, 2004), 72.

15. John Piper, *When the Darkness Will Not Lift* (Wheaton, IL: Crossway, 2006), 38.

16. Consider the Israelites when they were enslaved in Egypt for four hundred years. They cried out to the Lord for help but had no indication if God really heard them until Moses started performing

miracles. Even when it seems like God isn't listening or seeing, he is and he does (Exodus 3:7–9).

Chapter 11: God with Us
1. John 3:16–18.
2. Romans 6:5; 1 Corinthians 15:35–49; 1 John 3:2.
3. John 20:20, 27.
4. Hebrews 4:15.
5. Colossians 1:19.
6. Mark 4:12.

Chapter 12: Present for Absence
1. Romans 2:6, 12:17–19; 2 Thessalonians 1:6.
2. Genesis 3:21.
3. Matthew 27:51; Mark 15:38.
4. Another passage in Hebrews is similar to Hebrews 6:19–20 about the veil. Hebrews 10:19–22 says, "Therefore, brothers, since we have confidence to enter the holy places by the blood of Jesus . . . let us draw near with a true heart in full assurance of faith." I have often heard this verse used, as you may have, as a call to worship. We are told that we can draw near to God in worship and enter behind the curtain. You may have also heard Hebrews 4:16 quoted in a similar way: "Let us then with confidence draw near to the throne of grace." However, none of these verses are referring to a time of worship or an experience. These verses give us confidence to persevere to the end (4:14, 10:23), hope in Christ (6:18), and look forward to the day when we will be with Jesus in heaven (6:20; 10:25).
5. 1 Corinthians 15:19.
6. Romans 6:5, 8:23; 1 Corinthians 15:40–53.
7. Matthew 1:23.
8. Matthew 28:20.

Chapter 13: The Spirit and Absence
1. See Genesis 4:16; Numbers 14:42–43; and Psalm 10:1. For a detailed treatment of this idea, see John S. Feinberg, *No One Like Him: The Doctrine of God* (Wheaton, IL: Crossway, 2006), 250–51.

2. John 3:8.

3. Galatians 5:22–23.

Chapter 14: Sooner Than We Deserve, but Not As Soon As We Desire

1. 2 Peter 3:11–13.

2. Romans 6:5, 8:23; 1 Corinthians 15:40–53.

3. 1 Corinthians 15:35–44.

4. Anthony Hoekema, *The Bible and the Future* (Grand Rapids, MI: Wm. B. Eerdmans Publishing Company, 1979), 168.

5. This has always been God's plan. In Zechariah 14:9, we hear God's desire and promise that he "will be king over all the earth." See also: Genesis 3:8, 17:7–8; Exodus 6:7; Leviticus 26:12; Jeremiah 30:22, 31:33, 32:38; Ezekiel 11:20, 36:28, 37:27; Zechariah 2:10–11, 8:8; Hosea 2:23; 2 Corinthians 6:16; Hebrews 8:10; Revelation 21:3.

6. God will be so near that we won't need the sun or moon anymore because God himself will be our light (Isa. 60:19–20; Rev. 21:23, 22:5).

7. Romans 3:10, 23.

8. John Stott, *The Cross of Christ* (Downers Grove, IL: Intervarsity Press, 1986), 152.

9. Tertullian, quoted in Richard Watson, *Evidences, Doctrines, Morals and Institutions of Christianity* (New York, NY: T. Mason and G. Lane, 1836), 1:501. See also David Murray, *Jesus on Every Page* (Nashville, TN: Thomas Nelson, 2013), 76–77.

10. Clooney, *His Hiding Place Is Darkness*, 54.

ABOUT THE AUTHOR

David Bowden is an international speaker and performer known best for his craft of spoken word poetry. He has performed his poems all around the world for hundreds of thousands of people, and his videos have attracted millions of views online. David and his wife, Meagan, live in Oklahoma City, Oklahoma.